Spiral Blueprint

A Moving Meditation for Inner Peace

L. Bogedin

LONE MESA PUBLISHING
www.lonemesapublishing.com
ISBN 978-0692629314

Spiral Blueprint: A Moving Meditation for Inner Peace
Copyright Lori Bogedin, 2016

Table of Contents

Acknowledgments

The experience you are about to read is one that has profoundly and forever changed my life. I truly believe the words that create this story will make a difference in the lives of everyone who reads this book. So I would like to start by thanking you for trusting your intuition. May you read this with the full knowledge that you are a treasured gem, perfect in all you are and lovingly embraced within the Blue.

I want to take a moment to thank those who have helped me put my adventure into words. I have learned that writing a book is more a group activity than an individual endeavor.

So I want to thank, Ingrid Carson, from the bottom of my heart for her inspiring input, teamwork, and exceptional work. Without Ingrid, my story would never have been written and would still live only as pictures in my memory. Ingrid's innovative thinking, professional manner and personal way pushed this project to completion.

> *I know how hard you have worked, Ingrid, to ensure the presentation of my story is a success and sees its way to the next level. I hope you know how much your great work, effort, and friendship mean to me. Ingrid, as we enter the homestretch of this project, I hope you look at this body of work with pride, knowing that, in making my words coherent, you have profoundly changed at least one life—mine. I truly believe the words that create this story will make a difference in the lives of everyone who discovers the Blue. Thank you, Ingrid Carson, for a job well done! Your friend and admirer, Lori.*

I would also like to praise Teri Burns and Jennifer Phelps for their invaluable input, edits, and advice. Without them, this book would not have seen completion.

Thank you to all my friends and family that I forced, throughout the years, to listen to my story over and over again. I love you all for wanting to rediscover my tale—an adventure you already know all too well.

Prologue

My sincerest hope was to put into printed word, eBook and/or voice a life-changing experience I had with as much visual description as I could. I envisioned the words flowing easily from my crystal-clear memory of the event, which took place in my very early twenties. Now, forty-something-(cough, cough)-plus, I wanted the pages to be filled with epic images that allow you, my reader, to live the same exact experience I had. I wanted my words to paint such vivid pictures of this awe-inspiring, terrifyingly spiritual, yet beautiful, journey so that you would see and feel exactly what I had.

Let's cut to the chase and establish now what will soon be obvious—that when it comes to grand adventures, sometimes words fall short. For me, it's similar to trying to explain a first visit to, say, the Grand Canyon, which by the way I have never seen and can only imagine. So, when I tell you I was smaller than a grain of sand standing in what I can only describe as a cave-like cat toy, you must understand I have no other way of describing the experience. Yeah, you read it right, a cat toy! I mean the tubular circular thing that allows a cat to chase an enclosed ball around and around the outer opening, where the ball can be seen, but cannot get out.

Trying to tell others about what they themselves have never experienced is more difficult than I thought, but this is my attempt at doing just that.

Be assured that although my words are not as poetically striking as I had hoped, this is my effort to physically bring you into my experience with as much emotion and sense of inspiration as I had. My cat-toy cave now reminds me of the Large Hadron Collider (LHC)—the world's largest and most powerful particle accelerator. When I had this experience, there was no such device. With a description of something as grand as the LHC backing my story instead of a cat toy, perhaps it would not have taken me *25* years to write. I know now that I was held within my own energy field called a "torus," a pattern of energy that flows around each of our bodies in a circular pattern, much like an inner tube or life buoy. Understanding the torus, which is explained in more detail in Chapter Seven, is essential to my experience.

Before connecting with what I refer to as the Blue, I—like many people—suffered emotionally, cut off from any sense of my personal power. I was anxious, confused, and riddled with fears, not the least of which was the fear of death. My experience connecting with the Blue released all my fears—released it all. I had a new desire to fully embrace life and experience it in a meaningful and positive way. Compared with the darkness that had come before, this awakening was nothing less than a miracle for me. I didn't turn my life around and become healthy immediately. I didn't become rich overnight (damn!), or more beautiful (double damn!), and I still had to work at getting my life on track.

I was not without my previous struggles, but what I did have was the confidence to know it could and would be better. This transformation was more gradual, more natural, and WAY less dramatic than overnight, but it happened. Something did shift, and the immensity of what I experienced could never be unlearned. I was shown that every single thing is held within, made complete by, and will always exist in utter Unconditional Love—the Blue. And I began to act from that place and seek it again and again.

Since my experience, many things have happened and I have also made many other discoveries. The quality of pure love I saw and felt led me more and more in the direction of spirituality and energy work. With each new step, I was a little further from that well-worn difficult path. Today, I am an Ordained Spiritual Minister, an Intuitive Reiki Healer, and an IET Energy Healer. I am a life-student of the I Ching and I work with the energy messages of crystals. My husband and I own and operate a successful restaurant and have four beautiful children. As of writing this book, we also have a grandson who has without a doubt stolen my heart.

I am now equally fascinated by all religious and spiritual practices and modern science. I believe that these worlds are edging ever closer to one another. To me, it feels like the right time to share what I experienced and the meditative practice that intuitively evolved out of it. This meditative practice has helped me through many difficult times. But I am also not here to tell you that there is some magic practice that you can do or download or some treatment that takes away all of life's struggles. Sorry. I still have good days and bad days, but the bad times are shorter and easier to spot.

This book is structured in three sections that explain the experience I had in better detail. The sections coordinate with chapters that, one by one, give a step-by-step description of how to do the Spiral Blueprint Meditation and offer the science to back up what I believe occurred. Each chapter ends with additional and optional advice, meditations, and information. In Chapter Ten, you will find the complete meditation in motion.

Introduction

The vast, immense and grand tunnel in which I stand stretches on, seemingly endless. Very far into the distance and on either side of me, the tunnel appears to curl inward and around on itself, and huge openings line the outer wall.

Looking in either direction, I can imagine a ball as big as a planet rolling around the inside of this cat-toy cave, but I know no planet-sized, cat-toy ball is coming from either direction. The vast opening looks out into a never-ending stretch of space composed of pure color—Blue.

The Blue is love, pure and boundless. It is love without conditions, without expectations, without fear of loss and without end. It is love at its purest and it is everything and everywhere. I am given an implausible glimpse of Divine Unconditional Love.

The Spiral Blueprint Meditation was developed out of my desire to stay connected with the beautiful, all-loving dimension I experienced as the Blue. At the time I had the experience, I was in my early twenties and a young single mom working three jobs. I did not have the time to pursue a complete regular discipline such as yoga, Tai Chi, or long sessions of meditation. Frankly, I didn't even know there were such things. So over the years of trying to reconnect with the Blue, I evolved a meditation in motion that can be performed easily by anyone, no matter what your schedule is or even what your physical restrictions may be. The Spiral Blueprint Meditation will allow you to reconnect with life and help open up channels that may be blocking access to all levels of joy, positive attitude and, most of all, unconditional love. This meditation in motion can remove the rocks from any path.

Gregg Braden, international author, speaker and a trained scientist who now examines the relationships between what we believe and what we manifest, is a contemporary pioneer in bridging the

---

1 "Quoteworthy Science," APS News, http://www.aps.org/publications/apsnews/199904/quoteworthy.cfm.

worlds of science and spirituality. In his book *The Spontaneous Healing of Belief: Shattering the Paradigms of False Limits*, Braden maintains, "In the instant of our first breath, we are infused with the single greatest force in the universe—the power to translate the possibilities of our minds into the reality of our world."[2]

According to Braden, "Just the way sound creates visible waves as it travels through a droplet of water, our 'belief waves' ripple through the quantum fabric of the universe to become our bodies and the healing, abundance, and peace—or disease, lack, and suffering—that we experience in life."[3]

Today's quantum physicists understand that the world is not as solid or fixed, as it appears to be. Rather, it is composed of energy particles all constantly interacting with one another fluidly on many planes at once. There is no empty space. Absolutely all of it is filled with energy, and the energy of our minds and bodies is an active part of the greater fabric. In this way, we are bound to the Earth herself, just as we are connected to the upper etheric dimensions, which we do not always see with our eyes. Whether we see the Blue—or the Source, or the Matrix, or God, as it has also been called—we are energetically connected to it. In the same way, the Earth's iron core crystal echoes in the iron within our blood. These energetic entanglements cannot be broken, whether we choose to acknowledge their existence or not. It is up to us whether the connection works for us or against us.

The understanding that our thoughts and feelings not only have a profound effect on us but also affect the material world around us is a basic principle in many Eastern religions, as well as indigenous practices of yesterday and today. In such traditions, the individual's connection to the Earth as well as the upper etheric dimensions is honored and balanced through daily practices passed on to children from birth. In contemporary Western culture, however, we are given few if any tools for balancing and activating this powerful connection.

The last several thousand years of our human history serve as a painful example of our lacking ability to balance this connection. In astrological terms, we have been living in what is known as the Piscean Age, which has been defined by hierarchical structures and rigid thinking. As a species, we have mirrored the definition of the Piscean Age by moving away from a balanced and respectful relationship with Mother Earth to what is considered now as Modern Times. This can be seen in the rampant ecological destruction we have wrought. Instead of honoring the bountiful resources of Earth by maintaining a state of respectful interdependence, we have exploited and damaged Her to the breaking point. Not only that, the lack of flexibility in our thinking and belief systems has led to religious, racial, and sexual oppression, war, and even the horror known as genocide, a twentieth-century term that did

---

[2] Gregg Braden, The Spontaneous Healing of Belief: Shattering the Paradigm of False Limits (Carlsbad, CA: Hay House, 2008
[3] Ibid.

not exist before 1944.

On a personal level, many of us experience this terrible lack of balance in the form of depression, hopelessness, fear, chemical dependencies and so many more debilitating conditions. Before connecting with the Blue, I was suffering in a big way from a wide range of these, and at the time didn't realize how common this was for many people. So often it is tragically normal to feel trapped, immobilized, and uncertain about how to make our dreams become reality.

The good news is that the Piscean Age is drawing to a close, and the Aquarian Age is being ushered in. The exact moment is still being debated, but while the debate continues, we can be comforted knowing the crossover has already begun. We are indeed fortunate to be living in this transformational era, welcoming a new age characterized not by inflexibility and oppression, but by openness of thought and an increasing awareness of the interconnected nature of all things.

The reality of this transformation can be seen not only in the worlds of spirituality and astrology, but in the sciences as well. More and more physicists, astronomers, chemists, biologists and neuroscientists are making discoveries that reveal a flexible, entangled universe—one in which our thoughts, feelings, and practices have actual, quantifiable effects on the visible world.

In 1972, an American meteorologist named Edward Lorenz coined the now well-known phrase "the Butterfly Effect." The phrase comes from a paper Lorenz presented to the American Association for the Advancement of Science titled "Predictability: Does the Flap of a Butterfly's Wings in Brazil Set off a Tornado in Texas?"[4] Lorenz's findings indicated that, in essence, the answer to this question is yes. Tiny variations in a dynamic system ripple through the system, ultimately causing big changes later on down the line. This effect is not only true of weather systems, but seems to cross over into all areas of life. Even though today's scientists do not fully understand the unseen principles acting on our world, there is an ever-increasing awareness that the visible, physical world is connected to and affected by less tangible elements such as human consciousness and belief.

I believe that each of us has the power to raise our own awareness and tap into the fluid reality that surrounds us. We can each raise our personal vibration to discover a place of attunement with the energies of Mother Earth and the energies of the Divine Universe. In doing so, we can manifest change and create beauty in our personal lives on a daily basis. Not only that, we can kick off a Butterfly Effect that spirals out into the world around us, creating positive change on a global scale as well.

Whether you have been drawn to the *Spiral Blueprint* out of a desire to manifest change in your personal life or out of a wish to activate more balance and beauty in the world at large, your simple willingness to be here and to read this is already having a profound effect. All spirals of movement

---

[4] To read Lorenz's paper in its entirety, see http://eaps4.mit.edu/research/Lorenz/Butterfly_1972.pdf.

begin simply with a single, sincere intention. For this reason, there is no wrong way to engage with the Spiral Blueprint Meditation.

The nine simple motions of this Meditation are carefully designed to align your energy with both the pulse of Mother Earth and the spin of the creating universe. The Spiral Blueprint Meditation does not "create" a connection between you, the Earth, and the upper realms; that connection is there already and is permanent and cannot be broken. The Spiral Blueprint Meditation simply opens a clear path that activates a connection you already have and allows it to grow stronger. When I use the term *activate*, I am describing a permanent physical change that allows that which is entangled with the Blue to move freely. Quantum physics has demonstrated that the particles of our bodies and consciousness are tied up with the particles of the Earth as well as the larger universe. However, they may not be moving freely, which creates a feeling of stagnation—or a trapped feeling of being immobilized, blocked, or not flowing.

When you clear the pathway, the activated connection of your being can interweave with the Blue, blocked elements can move freely, and you begin to feel "in flow"—linked to all the dimensions rather than isolated or cut off from them. This is the place from which you can successfully manifest your dreams, desires, hopes, and intentions. The Spiral Blueprint Meditation is carefully designed to activate you by clearing your personal energetic space and keeping the energetic channels clear, helping you to travel a clear path of meaning, purpose, and possibility.

I will not promise you that the Spiral Blueprint Meditation is a cure-all for life's problems. Of course there will still be your own ups and downs. The difference for me is that I now move through the ups and downs with less struggle and fear, less self-blame and needless suffering. The *Spiral Blueprint* provides a resource and a practice to which you can return for peace of mind. Once you activate or reestablish your connection to the energies of Mother Earth and the energies of the All-Creating Universe, new possibilities for problem solving begin to present themselves, along with new opportunities for creativity and self-fulfillment.

My core motivation for writing this book is one that I believe you will share with me after reading it—when you experience the Blue, your natural connection to Universal Unconditional Love, you'll want to pass the experience along to others. When you receive a wonderful piece of good news that you know will bring comfort, peace, and strength to so many, you will be excited to share it. The beauty of it is you don't even have to pass the message along by talking about it if you don't want. Because of the Butterfly Effect, the simple act of raising your own vibration will ripple outward to raise the vibrations around you, in turn helping to raise the vibration of the entire planet.

If you are ready to get started with the entire meditation in motion, you can go straight to Chapter Ten and try it. Chapters Two through Nine offer more in-depth explanations for the purpose and meaning behind each of the individual motions, as well as supplementary exercises and meditations. These chapters can deepen your understanding of the Spiral Blueprint Meditation, why it was created and more about my experience with the Blue, but you don't have to read them all in order to get started. How you choose to interact with this book is up to you. With the Spiral Blueprint Meditation, there is no way to do it wrong.

Section One:

Very Far From Blue

My epic life-changing journey started far from the secure loving comfort of the Blue I spoke of earlier. In fact, at the time I had the vision, I was not a likely candidate for such an epiphany. I was a troubled young woman traveling a rocky path—drinking, acting irresponsibly, afraid of death and yet drawn toward self-destructive behaviors. I had become a single mother at the age of seventeen. My mother told me later in life that some people just need to take the harder path to find out where they are going. This was true for me.

The birth of my beautiful son was profoundly life-altering, and I desperately wanted to find a healthier way of being, for his sake as well as my own. But I had no idea how to begin, how to change direction. I travelled a well-worn path at this point. I did not have any regular spiritual practice and had no clue what that might even mean. I had no knowledge of Eastern philosophies, didn't know Zen from any other kind of Buddhism. If asked, I would have told you "The Age of Aquarius" was nothing more than a song from a sixties musical. I had never meditated or even taken a yoga class. My destructive lifestyle did, however, teach me to live in the now, but only for survival purposes.

It's not that I didn't care about finding guidance. I cared very much! I was a young mother who wanted to change my life so that my son didn't have to live my mistakes. In fact, I was actually desperate to find guidance, but I didn't know where to look. We had been raised "CE" (Christmas and Easter) Catholics, and as a young child, I sensed there was a greater presence and a greater purpose. I was often visited by what I thought of as my angel, who would comfort me during dark childhood times. I began begging my parents to take us to church more until, at a young age, I was told by a Sunday School Nun that "If you get an F in Sunday School class, you will have to explain it to Father and the entire church! And furthermore, see that dove in the stained-glass window? Well, if you ever think a bad thought about it, God will never forgive you because that is Jesus."

What do you think my very first thought was after she told me this? A bad one, of course! To the delight of my parents, I stopped begging for more church, and we were again practicing "CE" Catholics. That was good enough for them. Besides, the F thing was far too much pressure for a grade-school girl who could barely keep up academically in first- and second-grade public school.

In my early twenties, still seeking help and guidance, I again looked to traditional organized religion and found my spiritual home with the Methodist Church. With different degrees of Christian belief and acceptance, founder John Wesley declared, "We think and let think."[5] The Methodists required no beliefs in dogmas and imposed no particular mode of worship. In rural Northeastern Pennsylvania in the mid-1980s, the Methodist Church was the most forward-thinking and liberal system I could find.

For a while, I was able to find what I needed and truly came to love Jesus and still do. Baby Jesus is obviously the cuter Jesus, but nonetheless, he's still my main guy. Leonard Cohen once said, "There is a crack, a crack in everything; that's how the light gets in."[6] Perhaps my heart (or mind) was cracked opened just enough in my desperation, to receive any gift of insight. I turned to Christianity and was able to start rebuilding my life.

During this time, I had been praying for answers, a sign of some kind. That night, exhausted during a long third shift at the mental health residential group home where I worked, I lay down for a moment on the office couch. As the Bible says, *Ask and thou shall receive.*[7] I have come to call what happened to me that night an out-of-body experience, for lack of a better practical term. What took place was an experience of such magnitude that at age twenty-two, I…well, woke up! It was as if I had been shaken out of a very long, very dark sleep. For now, all I can say is that what happened changed my life absolutely, in an instant, and forever:

> *I am standing beneath a blazing hot sun in a barren, desert-like landscape. Every part of me feels burned, tattered, and sore. My lips are dry, but there is no moisture in my mouth to relieve the cracked skin. I can see, feel, smell—this is not a dream. It is as real as any waking hour. The earth beneath my feet is hard and dry. I am wearing old army-style boots that are too big for my aching, blistered feet. As I walk, they crumble the cracked earth and rub the sores on my feet with each step. The clothes on my body are ratty, war-torn rags, barely substantial enough to protect my skin from the blistering sun directly above me. The sky is a brilliant, cloudless blue, but there is no breeze—only the hot blazing sun. Within the fevered confusion of my brain, I can only imagine the cool, blue beauty of the sky in stark contrast to the desolation and sweltering heat of the*

---

5 John Wesley, "The Character of a Methodist," The Works of John Wesley (Thomas Jackson edition, 1872), http://www.umcmission.org/Find-Resources/John-Wesley-Sermons/The-Wesleys-and-Their-Times/The-Character-of-a-Methodist.

6 Leonard Cohen "Anthem," http://genius.com/2001798/Leonard-cohen-anthem/There-is-a-crack-a-crack-in-everything-thats-how-the-light-gets-in

7 Matthew 7:7.

landscape.

Complete silence surrounds me. Not even the slightest trace of a breeze stirs the stagnant air. The dry earth screams out for even a single drop of water, but there is none to be found. The air itself is parched, completely devoid of moisture, and burns my throat when I try to breathe. As I struggle to inhale whatever oxygen I can, I look around with eyes squinted against the glare of the sun. The heat ripples the air as it rises and distorts my vision. As I focus, I become aware that my surroundings are not as featureless as they first appeared. There are numerous bulges in the lifeless brown earth, each about the size of a small car. They swell up out of the cracked dirt, like boils on a sick and dying planet.

I realize that I am standing on top of a sloping hill or bald mountain, and these structures stretch out all around me to the horizon. There are thousands of them, maybe hundreds of thousands. Crooked and worn paths that seem to begin and end where I am standing, wind between them. I make my way down an uncertain path, dazed by the strangeness of my surroundings. Gradually, I become aware of the eerie sensation that I am being watched. I am not alone; I can feel it—and sense others. I feel the weight of hundreds of suspicious, anxious eyes. As I look around for some sign of these mysterious watchers, I see that the boil-like mounds of earth each have a small, dark opening at the top. They look like hungry mouths, open in a silent scream at the perception of coolness in the blue of the sky.

There is still no visible sign that anyone other than me is there, but somehow I know that each of these mounds is inhabited. Each of the inhabitants is watching me, and each of them is terrified and filled with a rage so deep it's tangible. A profound anger radiates from the fragile mud domiciles surrounding me on all sides, assaulting me with their terrible force.

As I walk the dusty strange path, I can only wonder who these scared and angry souls are who inhabit the poorly made mud huts. Their misery floods my body with a terrible fear and sadness. Then the smell hits me—an acid-sulfur mix of smoke and toxins assaults my senses, making it impossible to breathe. I gag and drop to my knees like a helpless child caught in a house fire. There is no oxygen, only poisonous fumes that tear at my throat and burn my lungs. I crawl along the ground, gagging, choking, and silently begging for help. The watchers do nothing. Their lack of compassion hits me like a boxer's final blow, knocking me completely to the ground. How many of them inhabit this desolate, dying world? How can they stand silently by, doing nothing as I struggle and plead? "Why won't anyone help me?" I vaguely wonder as I gasp for air. My cheek scrapes the hard surface of the lifeless ground.

Chapter One:
Stillness and Intention

"The present moment is all you ever have.
There is never a time when your life is not 'this moment.' Is this not a fact?"
— Eckhart Tolle[8]

Motion One: Stand with your feet shoulder-width apart, knees slightly bent, back straight, and arms at your side. If needed, you may sit in a chair with your back straight and arms resting at your sides or on your lap. Even if you are completely immobile, you can imagine the steps in your mind's eye. The effects will be the same. Your intention is to be in the present moment, in mind and body. Relaxing your mind and body, become aware of how you feel and of your surroundings. Become aware of your breathing in...and out.

The first motion of the Spiral Blueprint Meditation simply requires you to assume a comfortable posture and allow yourself to be still, while holding the intention of being in the present moment. Although it may not seem that you are doing very much in this first motion, stillness and intention are important in setting the stage for the rest of the meditation. Of course for most of us, being present in *this moment* can be much more difficult than it sounds!

Usually, we have a steady soundtrack of tasks, obligations, concerns, worries, and fears running through our minds, and these generally have more to do with the past or the future than with the present moment. If you find it difficult at first to be fully present, know that this is normal and do not judge yourself. Simply allow your thoughts to rise up, and then release them, returning your attention to your breathing.

The human brain is made up of two hemispheres, each serving a different function. The right hemisphere thinks in pictures, both specific and abstract. It takes in the information of the present moment through the senses, perceiving all we see, hear, smell, and touch at this moment. The right

8 Eckhart Tolle, The Power of Now: A Guide to Spiritual Enlightenment (Novato, CA: New World Library, 1999), 58.

hemisphere perceives the present moment, whereas the left hemisphere of the brain is responsible for organizing and categorizing these perceptions. The left brain thinks not in pictures, but in language. It is also responsible for linear thinking, including all our thoughts about the past and the future. That ever-present internal chatter, reminding us to do certain things, or expressing regret about the past or fear for the future, is a product of the left hemisphere of the brain.

When brain researcher Jill Bolte Taylor suffered a stroke that impaired the function of the left hemisphere of her brain, she experienced her own consciousness from the right-brain perspective only for a time. In her Ted Talks lecture, Taylor vividly describes what it felt like to stop thinking in a linear way and to lose the sensation of individual identity.[9] She could no longer differentiate the molecules of her own body from the molecules of the wall next to her. She experienced herself as enormous, unbounded energy connected to the universe. Taylor's experience highlights the degree to which our bodies are an illusion of sorts. The energy of which we are made is absolutely entangled with the larger universe; it's just that we're not always in touch with that. However, an awareness of this fact is what allows us to reclaim our connection with both the Earth and the upper etheric dimensions, allowing us to manifest our most cherished hopes and desires.

You are not your past or your future. You are not your thoughts, your emotions, your personality, your mistakes, successes, abilities, or beliefs. You are not even the body that houses your form. Like everything and everyone around you, you are universal life force energy. *Life Force Energy* is just what the name implies. It is the energy from the Source that animates and gives life to a physical body. Here on this material plain called Mother Earth, of course, we need our physical minds and bodies, too. We need our minds to create our thoughts and our thoughts to create our reality. The problem is that for most of our waking hours, the mind is left on autopilot, playing a soundtrack of past failures, present anxieties, and fears about the future. Learning to quiet this negative chatter is the first step toward tapping into the power we all have within our own minds: the power to create the beautiful reality we actually want.

When we are coming from a place of pain, experiencing trouble, lack of motivation, and frustration with our lives, it can seem impossible to find a place of stillness or to focus on a single intention. We may be drowning in hopeless feelings, unable to find the proper direction in which to focus our energies. As a troubled teenager, I was about as unfocused as a person could possibly be. I drank, partied all the time, and engaged in reckless behavior. I wanted desperately to either change or die, but didn't know how to do either. And I truly didn't want either.

9 Jill Bolte Taylor, "My Stroke of Insight," Ted2008,
http://www.ted.com/talks/jill_bolte_taylor_s_powerful_stroke_of_insight?language=en.

At that time, I would have laughed out loud at the idea of "finding stillness" or "developing a positive intention." In that place, I did not see how I had any power within me to change my life. But the fact is that I did have that power within me, held safely within the right hemisphere of my own brain. Before I could get there, I needed to still the buzzing hyperactivity of the left hemisphere. This is the power we all have as humans to reconnect with the divine energy of which everything is made. The reconnection begins here, in the present moment—which is all we really have.

In addition to being present in this moment, the first motion of the Spiral Blueprint Meditation also calls for you to hold an intention in your mind. This is not as complicated as it may sound. Your intention could be as simple as a single word like "love," or an affirmation such as "I believe in my own power to create change," but it doesn't even have to be this specific. Simply *intend to be present* for the Meditation. So bringing a smile to your face, even if you have to force it a little, could be your intention. This intention begins the process of activation, which I discuss in more detail later. You don't have to create the connection—or really "do" anything at all—just allow it to be, and be in the moment.

The work of Japanese energy scholar and water researcher Dr. Masaru Emoto provides an eloquent illustration of the true power of intention. For more than twenty years, Dr. Emoto has been working with water, examining the effects of various messages upon this highly expressive element. Over the years, Dr. Emoto and his researchers have exposed water samples to music, words, images, and thoughts, and then examined the frozen crystal structures beneath a high-powered microscope. The results are astounding. When water has been exposed to prayer or to words and thoughts such as *love*, *gratitude*, and *peace*, its crystalline structure is simply beautiful—a six-sided, unique, lacy snowflake, whose form is delicate, balanced, harmonious, and pleasing to the eye. However, when the water is exposed to negative and aggressive ideas such as *hate* or *disgust*, the frozen sample reveals only chaos, with distorted, unpleasant, even visually disturbing shapes that have no harmony or balance.

In the documentary *Messages from Water*, Dr. Emoto explains that everything in the universe is made up of energy and emits vibrations.[10] He believes that the water responds according to the vibrations traveling through it—good or bad. The water in the form of a beautiful structure, therefore, visibly expresses that which supports and honors Mother Nature's own designs. That which is not in balance with Mother Nature demonstrates the opposite. The implications of Dr. Emoto's research are enormous. For one thing, our bodies contain up to 60 percent water. Imagine what the crystalline structures of that water might reveal after a day full of hopeless thoughts or self-blame. What about after a day of peaceful meditation and self-acceptance? This is one reason why, in the first motion of

---

[10] To view Dr. Emoto's documentary, see http://www.cultureunplugged.com/play/8141/Messages-from-Water.

the Meditation, it is important to hold some type of positive intention in your mind, even if it is simply to be present.

The fact that Mother Earth can use water as a way of communicating messages to us is also evidence of the intricate and profound ways in which we are connected to Her. The spinning motion of the Earth sends our personal light vibration into the upper realms where thoughts and intentions manifest. The more we align ourselves with the spin of the Earth and find our own personal place of balance with that connection, the more beautifully and harmoniously our intentions will manifest in the world. We begin with finding a place of quiet and grounding ourselves to Her.

A Moment of Zen

This exercise can be done before the first motion of the Spiral Blueprint Meditation to help you become relaxed and present in what Eckhart Tolle calls "the Now."[11] It is not necessary to do this in order for the Meditation to work; it is simply an added technique that helps to bring your awareness into the present moment, quieting any left-brain chatter about the past or the future.

"Zen" is a word that gets thrown around a lot. If you look it up, you'll find that Zen applies to everything from yoga to art, and even to motorcycle repair. Part of the reason that Zen has achieved such widespread popularity is that it is, by definition, a concept not bound by words. It is a right-brain concept, like many Eastern philosophies such as the Tao. Tao (pronounced "dao") means "path" or "the way." It is a universal law or rule underlying everything from the creation of galaxies to the interaction of human beings. This is another area where Eastern and Western cultures differ.

Western languages are phonic, meaning that as you read this, the words are conveyed to your brain as sounds that correspond with their meaning. This is strictly a left-brain function. Many Eastern languages, on the other hand, are imagistic, being made up of many complex picture groupings. The pictures tell a story that is recognized and put into meaning by the right hemisphere of the brain. The process of interpretation is intuitive and symbolic.

Zen comes from the Japanese pronunciation of the Chinese character "chan." The word Chan comes from the Sanskrit word "dhyana." Dhyana can best be translated to mean a "meditative state or tranquil thinking." The Zen attitude has been developing, changing and evolving ever since human beings needed to enter into meditative states to find peace of mind. At some point in our evolution we became aware of the present moment as being different from the past or future. We also became distracted by the idea of "having," which gave rise to all kinds of illusory conflicts. As we became more

11 Tolle, The Power of Now.

interested in the material world, we spent less and less time experiencing our oneness with the Earth. This oneness is still understood and enjoyed by animals, and remains accessible to us. However, now we need to consciously enter a meditative state in order to experience it.

The following exercise is a quick, simple way to begin experiencing your own Zen state and can be performed pretty much anywhere, anytime you have a few minutes. First, read through the steps. Once you understand them, stop reading and spend about three minutes doing the exercise.

1. *Bring your awareness to each part of your body in turn. As you do so, simply notice how that part of your body feels right now. Try not to focus on why your body feels that way or whether you should do anything to change the feeling. Simply notice.*

2. *Begin with your feet. For example: Are your feet bare or housed in shoes, socks, boots, or perhaps a pair of Stuart Weitzman high heels (oh to dream...)? Where are your feet? On the floor or elevated?*

3. *Next, notice how your feet feel: Cold, warm, sore, comfortable?*

4. *Move your awareness upward through your legs, back, stomach, chest, arms, shoulders, neck and head, and simply notice how each part feels at this moment.*

5. *Take note of what is happening around your body right now. Using each of your senses in turn, simply observe:*
   - *What sounds can you hear?*
   - *What do you smell?*
   - *What sensations can you feel on your skin: wind, dampness, the fabric of your clothes?*
   - *What do you see around you: a tree, a chair, a wall, a painting, a lamp, flowers?*

Notice whatever is there, without judging or analyzing it.

If you focused only on *how* you felt and not *why* you felt that way, you were in the "Now." You were not questioning events of the past or projecting issues into the future. Like, "Will I ever own a pair of Stuart Weitzman high heels?" for example. The theory behind Zen is that the more you are in the present, the more you are in flow with the universe. This short exercise can be practiced anytime you have a few minutes, helping to bring your awareness into the present moment.

Chapter Two:
The Breath and the Body

"Remember, in our inmost being, we are all completely lovable
because spirit is love. Beyond what anyone can make you think or feel about yourself,
your unconditioned spirit stands, shining with a love nothing can tarnish."
— Deepak Chopra[12]

*Motion Two: Relax by taking three deep breaths, inhaling deeply and
exhaling slowly. With each exhale, relax your body from head to toe. If
necessary, keep taking slow deep breaths a little longer than three times.
Just breathe in and out until you are fully relaxed, jaw and shoulders soft,
and all tension is released throughout your entire body. As you breathe,
slowly become aware of the sounds around you. Notice the smells.
Become mindful of how you physically feel: peaceful and energized or in
pain and tired. Simply become aware—without judgment—of the
environment and how your body feels in this moment, but don't think
about the connections you have to these things. Relax and allow yourself
to simply be aware. If you feel yourself starting to think, judge or worry,
return your attention to your breathing. Focusing on even one breath
can help you to become mindful again.*

The last chapter addressed the challenge of coming into the present moment. One of the most useful tools we have in this quest is our breath. Our breath is our life force, the vital energy that flows through us at every moment from the moment of our birth. Most of the time, we are unaware of our breath, simply taking it for granted. When we attune to our breathing even for a moment, it helps us quiet the left-brain chatter about the past and the

---

12 Deepak Chopra, The Path to Love: Spiritual Strategies for Healing, (New York, NY: Three Rivers Press, 1997), 71.

future. Our breath is a tangible expression of our energy, and the medium through which we can bring ourselves into our bodies. When we become mindful and present in our bodies, we begin to sense our place in the energetic grid that makes up all life—the energy that loops through our bodies, down beneath our feet into Mother Earth, and then in a radiating orb around our bodies and into the upper etheric dimensions where our dreams and visions can manifest. Essentially this donut-shaped energy pattern, called the torus, is found everywhere and in everything—in atoms, cells, seeds, flowers, animals, trees, hurricanes, plants, the sun, galaxies, and even humans—flowing and then surrounding back into itself. The cosmos as a whole is surrounded by this infinite circulation, and absolutely everything has its own toroidal electromagnetic field.

The second motion of the Meditation is about turning your attention to the precious flow of breath within your body, and allowing the simple, nonjudgmental awareness of this flowing life force to call your mind into the present moment. This reminds you to leave the activities of your left-brain thinking—self-judgment and self-cruelty—behind. Self-judgment comes largely from clinging to the past and projecting anxiety and fear into the future. The Blue *does not judge*. Universal Unconditional Love—that matrix that binds all that is—*cannot judge*.

You did not always judge yourself, either. Remember when you were a baby? Since we only begin developing concrete, easily recallable "memories" around the age of two, you might not remember clearly. Your body remembers, though. Those earliest days are embedded within your very cells. But whether you consciously remember it or not, the point is this: when you were a baby, you knew what you needed, and you did not judge yourself for having those needs. If you needed food or dry clothes or safety, you let someone know by crying. And you didn't judge yourself for having or expressing those needs. There was no such thing as doubt. You acted instinctually to make sure that your survival needs were met.

Of course, as we grow and become aware of our ability to make decisions, things get more complicated. Perhaps the careless comments of others, painful childhood experiences or negative input from everything around us began to introduce judgment and anxiety into our experience of the world. Perhaps, you have even felt that you impacted others in a negative way. But just because your perception has changed does not mean the core reality has changed.

Unconditional Universal Love is everything. It is the glue holding together what appear to be the empty spaces between things. The Spiral Blueprint Meditation reconnects you with that fact, helping you release your own personal barriers to fulfillment. You can reconnect with your innate instinct, with the trust and belief that your needs and desires can and will be met from a place of unconditional love. You are unbounded, brilliant, divine energy, connected to everything and capable of anything you wish.

But what on this plane of existence contains that energy? Your body, like everything else, has an energy pattern that is vital to the universal energy grid. When directed properly, the energy you are made of can plug right into the energy of Mother Earth and the Divine Universal Energy. This connection and communication is the natural state of things. When we find our own place of balance within it, we experience the deep joy that is our birthright. We begin to see our most precious hopes and dreams manifest around us. This is the universe's gift to us.

All too often, we are unable to connect with the gift we are offered. Unfortunately, the norm in contemporary Western culture is to live in a chronic state of stress, self-judgment, and anxiety, which is often compounded with feelings of shame and lack of self-confidence. This was how I felt every day before I made contact with the Blue. My thoughts were generally anxious and fearful, rather than positive and hopeful. I needed a major life-changing experience to show me there was an entirely other way of being, and it was actually all around me. I was plugged into it whether I was aware of that fact or not!

Thankfully, it is not necessary to have a sudden out-of-body experience in order to connect with our natural state. Through presence and awareness within our own bodies, we can release our minds and hearts from toxic belief patterns. Negative, toxic beliefs are not abstract ideas. They are literal and physical, actually present within the chemistry of the brain. The transfer of neurotransmitters such as dopamine and serotonin allows the brain to activate potential change. However, our brain chemistry can just as easily *get in the way* of change.

If we allow our brains to run on autopilot, the chemical information delivery system is controlled by the subconscious. If the subconscious is repeatedly preoccupied with a negative, anxious thought pattern, the negativity creates a pathway within the brain that actually becomes ingrained. The more you travel the same negative path, the more likely you will default to negative or hopeless thinking. As a teenager and into my early twenties, I repeatedly walked the same troubled path and had worn such a deep groove of self-destructive behaviors that I couldn't step off. Even though this is a simplistic way of looking at the complex pathways of the brain, it is essential to engage the body as well as the mind when seeking to transform because the messages being delivered throughout your body are actually concrete *and* physiological. The mind and body work together in order to produce real, deep and lasting change. The more your mind and body work together, the more you will see your thought patterns become free to change. New opportunities and possibilities will open up in your life, as well as new options, ideas, and choices. Perhaps these opportunities were always there, but when you engage both mind and body, you are now traveling a different path and can see things from a different perspective! This can open up what seems like a whole new world.

You have the power to rewire your brain's neural pathways in a positive way, making it easier to initiate meaningful change. The more you reconnect with your natural state—one of unconditional love and peace—the more your brain's pathways change and open. You begin to see other ways of getting from Point A to Point B, rather than just using the same old habitual pathway. As you can imagine, this opens up radical new potential for growth and change in every area of your life. This is because you are actively correcting and restoring the very chemistry of your brain.

There is a beautiful legend I have always loved that comes from the Lakota Sioux tradition:

> The Creator gathered together all of Creation and said, "I need to hide something very important from the humans. Unlike you, they are young and do not realize that the present moment is all they have and that they create their own reality within these moments. This is strong medicine and must be hidden well, for humans are very curious. This medicine must only be found when they are ready and can use it to heal."
>
> The powerful Eagle said, "Give it to me, I have powerful wings and can fly it to the moon."
>
> The Creator said, "No. One day they will go there and find it."
>
> The smart and caring Dolphin said, "My tail is powerful, I will swim and bury it on the bottom of the ocean."
>
> The Creator said, "No. They dive deep into the oceans and will find it there, too."
>
> The mighty Buffalo stood strong and said, "I will bury it deep, out on the Great Plains."
>
> The Creator said, "They will cut into the skin of the Earth and find it even there. This must be a place that every human will find, but only when ready."
>
> Very hesitantly the small and meek Mole, who had no physical eyes and who lived in the breast of Mother Earth for protection, softly said, "Put the knowledge within them."
>
> The Creator of all that is bowed low with love for the small creature

and said with a smile, *"My small child who sees with spiritual eyes, it is done."*[13]

Here on Mother Earth, the body is the container for the spirit. Within us, we carry the knowledge and the ability to create our own reality. The breath is our birthright, a brilliant manifestation of the life force energy connecting our bodies to the greater universe and the source of our creation. By allowing the breath to bring us into our bodies, we can become gradually more and more attuned to the Source, the Creator, or the Blue.

It is not always possible to be in the present or to silence the negative internal chatter. Of course not! We are only human. However, it is something that comes more easily over time as we practice mindfulness or the act of being aware. The breath can work as a natural focusing tool, helping us to become present in our bodies. This should not be seen as a challenge, but as an opportunity. Even if the internal chatter is difficult to silence on a given day, accept that you are doing your best, and then turn your attention to your breath, exhaling judgment and inhaling the natural, cleansing truth of Unconditional Universal Love. More and more, you will begin to find your place within the divine energy grid, where you are wholly accepted and wholly loved.

A Breath of Fresh Air

The following is a simple breathing awareness exercise you can practice almost anywhere or anytime throughout your day. You can do this for one minute or as long as you wish. Like each of the supplemental exercises in this book, it is not necessary to practice it in order for the Spiral Blueprint Meditation to work. This is just an additional technique to help you become present in your body using the natural resource of your own breath.

1. *Close your eyes and turn your attention to your breath. At first, simply notice your breath, allowing it to flow in and out of you naturally, at your own pace. Do this for a minute or so.*
2. *On your next inhalation, draw a long, steady breath deep into your lungs. Fill your lungs from the bottom upward, from deep in your belly to the top of your throat. At the top of the breath, hold the breath for a*

---

[13] Adapted from http://ancientearthwarriors.com/tag/sioux-legend/.

count of 1-2-3-4. Now, slowly release the breath from the top down, emptying your lungs slowly from throat to belly. Visually, it is helpful to picture in your mind's eye a tall glass being filled to the top with water, then the glass being tilted and slowly emptied. Any time you are having trouble keeping your focus on the breath, repeat this visualization of the glass being slowly filled with water and emptied.

3. *Return to your own natural pace of breathing for a moment, gently noticing the natural rise and fall of your chest. As you do so, take a moment to express gratitude for the precious gift of your breath.*

Steps 2 and 3 may be repeated as many times as you wish. Be sure to end the exercise with a moment of gratitude for the wonderful, life-giving resource that is your own, unique breath.

Chapter Three:
Gifts from Gaya

Waken Mother Earth, Great Mystery,
teach me how to trust.
Teach me to trust my heart,
my mind,
my intuition,
my inner knowing,
the senses of my body,
the blessings of my spirit.
Teach me to trust these things
so that I may enter your Sacred Space
loving beyond my fears, taking only what is needed,
giving back more than I take, acting always in gratitude,
and thus walk in balance
with the passing of each glorious Sun.
—Lakota Prayer[14]

Motion Three: *Bring your hands up slowly from the sides of your body, cupping your palms up in front of you, with elbows slightly bent. Visualize pulling up two handfuls of the energy of Mother Earth, the way you would scoop up a draught of water in your cupped palms. Hold the energy out and up slightly as an offering. As you make this gesture, imagine you are pulling from deep within Mother Earth all her strength, calmness and restorative energy. Give thanks for her gifts.*

---

14 Adapted from https://yourdailyprayer.wordpress.com/tag/lakota/.

In the loneliness of personal suffering, the heat of stress and anxiety of life, or the toxicity of certain relationships, we tend to forget that Mother Earth provides all that we need and asks for nothing in return. During hard or stressful times, we become cut off from positive available resources and cannot see the options in front of us. This is the very definition of hopelessness, a feeling I am sure anyone can relate to. It is the stagnant, motionless state of existence where it seems there are no available options. When we enter a situation feeling isolated and/or forsaken, it's hard to see that there are always options! This step of the Meditation calls our awareness to the availability of Mother Earth's gifts. We take our rightful place in the divine energy field when we express gratitude for these resources, and we can do so knowing nothing will be asked of us in return.

It is no secret that in today's world, the Earth is suffering. In most cultures of the present era, the connection between our planet and ourselves is not emphasized or honored. Ecological imbalance manifests itself all over the Earth in the form of toxic waters, exhausted resources, poisoned air, and stripped-down forests. This chapter began with a traditional Lakota prayer as a reminder that, within many traditions of our past and some surviving in the present, a respectful relationship with Mother Earth is the norm. In the prayer above, the relationship between the speaker and the Earth is characterized by the understanding of our interdependence. The Earth is our grounding point—the place where we can find balance— and it is the source of all our resources and gifts on the material plane.

The first two motions of the Spiral Blueprint Meditation focus on bringing your awareness into the present moment and into your body. In this third motion, your energy begins the process of looping downward and connecting with the grounding force of Mother Earth. In this way, you begin a reactivation or rediscovering of the connection that has always existed.

As you practice the Meditation, a feeling of abundant gratitude will emerge naturally. This is because you are realigning with your natural state, which includes a profound gratitude for the gifts given both by Mother Earth and the Creating Universe. When you align with the three contact points of the Spiral Blueprint Meditation—you, the Earth, and the Divine Universe—love, service, and gratitude come naturally.

The number three is a very powerful number. This is reflected everywhere you look, from the Christian Holy Trinity to the importance of the triangle shape in nature. The conductive properties of quartz crystals are related to their pyramidal shape. This is because interaction among three sides or three things creates movement. When dealing with only two objects or energies, balance may be achieved, but it will be static. It will lack movement. The third object or energy creates an interaction among energies, leading to flow and activation. *The connection among these three points exists whether you are aware of it or not, and it can never be broken.*

It is important to know you already hold this connection within your being. The motions in the Meditation are only giving you a way to clear a new path. In practicing the Spiral Blueprint Meditation, you are simply bringing your awareness and intention to this interaction of energies so you can take your rightful place among them. This will change your world and quite possibly the entire world as a whole. Yes, you are that important! Our physical connection to Earth is not just symbolic or abstract. It is literal.

Scientists understand the center of the Earth is composed of an iron crystal. Quantum physicists are now finding that the Earth's core pulses with the energy of the universe, which reverberates in the blood running through our veins. In a very real sense, we are entangled with the spinning motion of the Earth and the entire universe. When we bring our individual awareness to this fact, we experience our connection to the pulse of Mother Earth on a conscious level. This connection loops into the spin of the creative aspect of the universe, allowing us to activate anything we wish. When we combine a practice of releasing fear, stress, and anxiety with a practice of embracing affirmation and gratitude, the energy flow moves in a positive direction; the bad flows out and the good flows in. From this place, we have room to create. When our vibrations become raised in this clear and healthy manner, we can reconnect naturally with the Blue, our natural state of being.

As we move into the coming Age of Aquarius, we can anticipate an incredible awakening of consciousness. But this awakening cannot happen on the etheric plane only! It must be grounded to Mother Earth, for this is the reality we are here to experience now. We cannot do it without being aware of our surroundings. The third motion of the Meditation calls you to an awareness of your natural connection with the energy of Mother Earth. As you cup your hands and visualize scooping up Earth's abundant gifts and resources, you are simply engaging your body so you trigger your connection with Earth—the natural and unbreakable connection that exists anyway. In doing this, you provide the foundation for the permanent loop to be opened between the three contact points of the Meditation: the Earth, you, and the Divine Universe.

As wonderful as it sounds, it is not always easy to feel in harmony with nature and grateful for the gifts of Mother Earth. In life, it can be a real challenge. This is because we may lack relationship with Mother Earth, and we may also simply lack the time! In my professional and volunteer life, I manage a lot of different projects. Like many people, I sometimes get so caught up in rushing from one thing to the next I forget to notice the gifts of Mother Earth that are right in front of me. My inner motto has always been, *A person needs to work hard and always be prepared.* I still believe this, but I also know there is room for more.

My sister once told me she makes it a point to notice something beautiful in nature and then tell another person about it. One day she told me about a bird she had recently seen. She described how pretty the bird looked perched in a beautiful tree on a perfect, bright morning, how the clouds looked, and how the sun caught the color of the bird and the tree. But she wasn't out in nature when she noticed this—she was stuck in a traffic jam!

Our lives can be crazy busy, there is no denying that. Nature itself can be a free and readily available wonderland that can boost your energy, relieve your stress, and calm your nerves. Accessing it is as simple as slowing down—or stopping dare I say—to notice. The more we notice the beauty of nature, the more energized, relaxed, and connected we become. Mother Earth is our physical home and she has decorated it for us to enjoy. The walls and floor and ceiling of this home are filled with beautiful sights, sounds, and smells. Not only does nature provide for our physical resources, it fills our emotional needs as well. Taking a moment to appreciate the beauty in nature relieves stress and grounds us to the Earth, the welcoming home for our bodies and spirits.

Awareness of Big Mama Earth

Here are a few simple things you can do to enjoy the gifts of Mother Earth, and you don't have to keep them to yourself. Share your moments of appreciation with others to bring a little positive, stress-relieving energy into their day.

1 Notice and Tell
One of the things my sister taught me is that you don't have to allow for a lot of free time in order to appreciate nature. It is something you can bring into each of your days, no matter how busy you are, and you don't have to go on a long nature hike to do it. My sister would use the time she spent driving into town to really notice (while driving safely, of course!) the beautiful Pennsylvania country scenery.

If you live in the city, notice a tree-lined street or rooftop garden. If you are doing some highway driving, take note of the landscape or perhaps a beautiful cloud formation in the sky. Or simply notice a flower box someone has planted—that is, after all, why he or she planted it!

2 Get Out Into It All
When you do have a little free time, why not spend it outside? Take a weekend hike or walk in the park. Don't have weekend time? Use a few minutes of your lunch break to stroll around the block or park or eat in an outdoor café. While you are out there in nature, use the time to really look around you and notice the beauty the world has to offer, then go tell someone!

3 Buy a Potted Plant or Flower or Look Out the Window

Even if you can't get outside, you can bring nature to you. Get a potted plant or flower, or have someone bring you one. Or simply look out of the window and take note. Even a rainy or snowy day has natural beauty. Spend a few conscious moments everyday observing some aspect of nature that is pleasant to your eyes and/or ears.

Don't forget to share what you see, hear and feel with someone else! If you make this a habit, you are going to get excited about all the restorative powers of nature and want to share. Trust me! It may sound weird to you now, but sharing will get others excited too. That's a win-win, energy-boosting, tree-hugging, and living-life habit! Enjoy the world today—and don't forget you can bring your camera along!

Section Two:
Life Before Blue

As my cheek scrapes the ground, I suddenly realize the watchers feel angry and something even worse as they look at me—I know they pity me. The awareness of their pity floods me with pain. A deep and terrible sadness overwhelms me, and I begin sobbing uncontrollably and am now filled with a profound hopelessness. Finally, I lift my head off the ground and realize I can feel nothing, not the hot blistering sun or the painful emotions—nothing. Nothing is worse than being terrified. Feeling nothing means hopelessness is all that is left. I lower my head back to the ground and offer my tears to the dry earth. My tears streak down, cooling my sunburned cheeks, and fall to the barren ground. They are pitifully little to offer such dryness. For a moment, my eyes take in the beautiful, clear blue of the sky again and then drift shut. I remember how I had once loved the sun, the hot summer days filled with the warm innocence of childhood. Now I long for the searing sun to go down, for cool night to come and cover me in darkness. A memory drifts through my aching mind: I am very young, in bed at night, and afraid of the dark. How ironic that now I am praying for the dark when once it had been so terrifying! I was always afraid of being alone in the darkness as a child.

But I was never really alone, I think as I lay weak and hopeless in the midst of this empty, burning world. I remember how I used to reach my tiny hand out from under the covers at night. "Are you here?" I asked. The reply always came. "Yes," the soft, sweet voice said, and a warm, strong hand would take mine, comforting me and taking away all my fear. "Why are you here?" I asked. The answer was always the same, "You are never alone." I remember falling asleep many nights holding that hand. I know now whose hand it was. Even though I was told it was my imaginary friend, I always knew differently. With a child's pure heart, I believed I was never alone and so…I simply wasn't.

Now, as I'm being watched and pitied, I lie in the cruel sun of a dusty, dead *planet and I long to go home. I yearn to be that small child again, safely held by my silent protector, my "angel." I cannot find my way forward in this terrible dead place, lying on the scarred, burnt ground. This is where my epic journey begins, far from the Blue. I am lost, crying out for help, but without the right words and without someone to listen. To whom can I extent my hand?*

I was fairly young the first time I tasted alcohol. Barely a teenager, I took a sip of one of the adults' leftover drinks during a Christmas dinner party at my grandparents' home. A warm, wonderful feeling came over me with that sip.

There were no parents screaming or crying or fighting. All I could hear were the adults chatting happily away and laughing, Christmas music played in the background and the fireplace was lit. With that first sip, I was instantly warm, I felt safe, and even the Christmas lights looked prettier. I felt peaceful and happy. It was magical. I remember thinking this is the most wonderful evening ever! I remember wishing every day could be like this.

Alcohol seemed to recapture that comfort and security from early childhood when my angel would visit me. Times with my angel were rare occasions I felt safe and cared for. What had happened to the all-loving, safe presence that would hold my hand at night when I felt lonely and afraid? As childhood became a thing of the past, so did the knowledge I was never alone. My angel was gone, and I was desperate for comfort.

As a young adult, I desperately attempted to find something that would comfort the miserable and lonely feelings that followed me like a lost, sad dog. But I did not have enough resources, and quite honestly I had no interest in seeking out professional help. At the time, it seemed easier and more fun and exciting to seek out unhealthy relationships, unhealthy activities, and unhealthy substances.

I started partying as soon as I could sneak out of the house. I didn't realize how hurt, scared, and lonely I really was. I just knew that when I drank, I seemed to feel happy. In my confusion, I also turned to boyfriends for comfort and soon became pregnant at age seventeen. My son was a beautiful gift, and his presence made me want to change directions even more desperately. But now I had much more complex adult problems. I had lost most of my friends to college or their still-active social lives. There would be no finishing college for me, and I had no work experience or job skills. I was no longer the reckless party girl everyone wanted to hang out with; I was a teenage mother in need of a job.

Determined to give my son a life he would be happy in, I eventually stopped drinking. I found the best job I could working the graveyard shift at a residential rehabilitation home. I lived at home with my recently divorced mother, my younger sister, and my son. The addition of a new life brought a new kind of joy into the house.

Our life was not a bad life, and in many ways I was lucky considering the circumstances. Still, I knew there must be more—more than just struggling to get by, more than being a single mother who was alone and relied on her parents for help. Something—an indefinable something—gently tugged at my mind, something I had once known but had forgotten, hovering there, waiting to be recalled. Even though my drinking had stopped and I had a sweet new life to care for, I was still the same lost, scared, insecure person.

My inexplicable journey began with a nightmare—delivering me to this aching, dying desert world, a place without comfort or hope. And then, as my tears fell onto the ground, I remembered that simple gesture from childhood, so long forgotten. I did the only thing I could think of—I reached out my hand.

Chapter Four:
There is Much We Do Not See

"To the dull mind all nature is leaden.
To the illumined mind the whole world burns and sparkles with light."
— Ralph Waldo Emerson[15]

Motion Four: While you are holding your cupped hands up, offer the gifts of Mother Earth and your gratitude to the Universe. Visualize brilliant colors—red, orange, yellow, green, blue, and purple flowing into your cupped hands from the creative center of the galaxy. Once your cupped hands are filled to overflowing, the intense colors transform into a luminous white light that overflows, like a waterfall from your hands. Both the energies—the energy from Mother Earth and the brilliant creative energy of the Divine Universe—mix and fall back to Mother Earth through their most powerful conductor: you. Give thanks to the Universe for this energy.

The last chapter focused on the gifts of Mother Earth. As your connection to the Earth is activated, your connection to the upper etheric dimensions is also activated. The fourth motion in the Spiral Blueprint Meditation is about visualizing these connections. The resources of Mother Earth can more readily be seen with the eye, and are more tangible due to the dense slower vibrations of the Earth. The energy of the Divine Universe is perhaps less tangible with its fast lighter vibrations, but it is no less real. In the fourth motion of the Meditation, we acknowledge the Divine Universal Energy as well, which is not something we can always see with our eyes. Nonetheless, it is here, all around us, at all times.

Everything in the world is part of a large energy field, in which all is connected. Remember, the Spiral Blueprint Meditation clears and reactivates the permanent, unbreakable link that exists among

---

15 For more quotes from Ralph Waldo Emerson, see http://www.goodreads.com/quotes/14250-to-a-dull-mind-all-of-nature-is-leaden-to.

the three contact points: you, the Earth, and the Divine Universe. In this fourth motion, visualization helps to draw your awareness to the connection between these energies. The known light spectrum is enormous, and all we can visually see with our eyes is just one-thousandth of a percent of it. The diagram below provides a striking illumination of this fact:

Diagram 1. Visible Light Spectrum

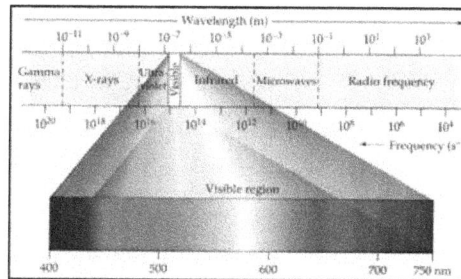

Source: Advantage Business Media,
http://www.ecnmag.com/article/2013/05/evolution-light-sensor-integration.

As Emerson's words at the beginning of this chapter suggest, the possibilities we see around us depend upon the quality of our vision—do we have a dull mind or an illumined or illuminated mind? What are we allowing ourselves to see? If you look at the concrete world around you, you can find numerous examples of the "dull mind." We see it in our overtaxed planet, our stressful lifestyles, the hopeless feeling that creeps into our daily lives. We are emerging from an age in human history that has been defined by science and technology to the tragic exclusion of transcendent vision and intuitive wisdom. Energetic attunement and broadness of vision has not been valued as much as so-called "cool reason."

For many sensitive people on the planet today, this is a very difficult world in which to live. We often feel trapped, not only as individuals but also as an entire species. The answers can seem impossible to find, and on the worst of those dull, gray days, it feels as if we are on an irreversible path toward destruction. If you are dissatisfied with any area of your life, you are probably hanging on to concerns, worries, and preoccupations. Subconscious negative thought patterns directly affect the quality of your energy and limit your ability to move or to flow. And when I talk about your "energy," I am not being poetic. We are, literally, luminous bodies of light. Thanks to the research of Marco Bischof, author of *Biophotons—The Light in Our Cells*,[16] we are beginning to understand this energy is very real and, with the proper instruments, it is actually visible.

Biophotons are weak electromagnetic waves in the optical range of the light spectrum that are

---

[16] Marco Bischof, Biophotons—The Light in Our Cells (Frankfurt, Germany: Zweitausendeins, 1995).

emitted by all biological entities. The living cells of plants, animals and humans all emit biophotons. Though invisible to the naked eye, they can be picked up with the latest equipment developed by German researchers. Specifically, biophoton light is found in our DNA molecules. Bischof's research indicates biophotons form a complex, dynamic communication network among the cells and tissues of our bodies. They may be the regulating agents not only for our physical systems, but also for non-physical systems such as memory and consciousness.

What does this mean? It means we can now see the Ch'i energy that flows in the meridian channels of our bodies. It means we are pure light energy. Our energy can actually be seen as a torus, or ring-shaped pattern. It extends out and around our bodies, rising through the crown chakra and then looping outward onto itself for about an arm's length and about a foot into the ground of Mother Earth before it loops inward and up again through our spine. This light spins and radiates in cycles. The Spiral Blueprint Meditation activates us by engaging the conscious mind with this dynamic, ever-present process. This may sound like a tall order and you may be asking, "What does it all mean for me, personally?" Is it feasible that the key to changing the future might not be so easy to see, held just short of our visual range? Is it also possible to change the world by changing our vision?

The transformation begins with us as individuals. So much human suffering is the result of hanging on to things, both material and emotional. Happiness comes from inside us. We often forget that and spend a lot of time blaming others for our unhappiness or seeking happiness outside ourselves. Attachments to material things, bad relationships, and mood-altering substances have become the norm in our society. Is this because we see so much that we have come to think of it as our reality?

The Spiral Blueprint Meditation permanently opens the energy loop of Unconditional Love, Service, and Gratitude. It connects the Divine Universe, the Earth, and you. Allowing yourself to reconnect on all levels integrates you with the positive energy flow of the Divine Universe. You are inherently a natural extension of this energy anyway. When you are at your best, free of negative belief patterns, this energy flows through you unhindered. By activating this connection and keeping your own energetic channels clear, you can take your place as a beautifully functioning expression of this energy and then everything you do becomes an extension of it as well. Not only does this benefit you personally, it benefits the entire world.

The Karo people of Peru, the last tribe of the Inca Nation, have held an ancient prophecy for centuries. The prophecy speaks of the return of "Patacutia," a word whose meaning combines "the turning over of the Earth" with the concept of "the Luminous Ones." According to the Karo people, with the return of Patacutia, Mother Earth will be restored to her former grace and beauty. What if I were to tell you that you are the vital link to the solution that will transform the world? What if I told you that all you had to do was shift your perception and see the universe for what it is—a living system. Every living system needs healthy essential parts to make it whole, meaning every man, woman, child, animal, and plant. What if each of us carries the potential to take our place on and with the Earth as a Luminous One? Perhaps all we need to do is open our eyes and broaden the scope of our vision.

You are a part of the oneness that is needed to start a change in the collective global mind. What if your connection could speed up the change in humanity so rapidly as to avoid total destruction? This is the Butterfly Effect. Would you still look at your life, your health, and your purpose the same way? We are all alchemists. We each have the potential to transform our reality, our world, and ourselves. More and more, this reality can be seen at the intersections of science and spirituality.

In Gregg Braden's book *The God Code: The Secret of Our Past, the Promise of Our Future,* the internationally renowned author and pioneer in bridging science and spirituality describes how a coded message has been found within the molecules of life and argues that every human being has the name of creation literally embedded in his or her DNA.[17] Braden's research uses Gematria, a methodology for converting words and phrases into numbers by calculating the sum of the letter values. This technique assigns numerical values to each letter of the Hebrew alphabet. According to Braden's logic, the basic elements of our DNA—hydrogen, nitrogen, oxygen and carbon—directly translate into specific letters of the Hebrew alphabet. These letters are YHVA and are believed to be the original translation of the name of God. Braden believes this code may be read as a timeless message to humanity, informing us of our capacity to heal and ultimately have peace on Earth. Our bodies are the sacred vessels of transformation. Like the caterpillar on the cusp of transforming into a butterfly, we are on the verge of becoming something greater than we are or have been. As a species, we can rise above materialistic concerns, above past and future, even transcend time and space.

If it is written in our DNA that we are The Luminous Ones that light up Mother Earth, can you still see humankind as dreadful, your life as hopeless, or the world as doomed? Or can you now see that all that is needed is the foresight of those who are willing to lead?

Visualization does not come easily for some. It is an activity of the right hemisphere of the brain: the visual, non-linear side. For those who tend to spend a great deal of the day in the left hemisphere, visualization can be a bit of a challenge. The left hemisphere is not used to seeing in pictures or abstract forms. As you practice the Spiral Blueprint Meditation, the visualizations will come more and more readily to mind. And remember, this is not a contest! If it is your intention to engage with the Meditation, there is no wrong way to do it.

---

[17] Gregg Braden, The God Code: The Secret of Our Past, the Promise of Our Future (Carlsbad, CA: Hay House, 2004).

A Visualization Exercise

As a preliminary practice exercise, try the following visualization:

In your mind's eye, see yourself reaching out and opening the door you use the most to enter your home. When you have a good and detailed picture of your front door, your hand on the doorknob of the door, imagine opening the front door and walking to your refrigerator. Now picture yourself opening the refrigerator door and taking out an orange. Feel the texture of the orange and smell the sweet oil of the fruit's skin. See yourself picking up a knife and cutting the orange into smiles. Feel the knife cutting into the orange and the juice on your hands. Pick up an orange smile and put it into your mouth and bite it so that when you smile your teeth show the skin of the orange.

There, you have just visualized! This is an activity we have probably all done, either as a child or with a child. And, if you are not a fan of oranges, you can do the exercise with any food you happen to love in your refrigerator!

Right-Brain Relaxation

The next exercise is something you may do if you simply wish to encourage right-brain activity and practice visualization. This exercise can be done lying down, sitting, or standing. It can take as much or as little time as you need. As you become more used to relaxing, it will take less time to enter the relaxed state.

1. *Choose a comfortable position and close your eyes. Relax every muscle in your body beginning with your toes and moving upward one muscle at a time through your feet, legs, pelvis, stomach, chest, shoulders, arms, neck, jaw, eyes, head, and face. Continue to breathe deeply and regularly at a comfortable pace.*
2. *When you think you are relaxed, release another layer of tension all over your entire body.*
3. *Move your awareness over your body again from toe to head. Wherever you sense tension, allow yourself to release it.*

4. *Repeat the entire relaxation three times. Each time you begin to think, "I am as relaxed as I can get," let go of another layer of tension.*
5. *Now, feel where you are in the space—physically and mentally. Feel your connection with Mother Earth. Where does your body touch solidness and where does it come into contact with air?*
6. *In your mind's eye, visualize yourself expanding like a firework in all directions, deep into the Earth and out into space at the same time. Like a rubber band, snap yourself back into your body.*

Repeat the last step several times, becoming huge and encompassing everything, then snapping back into your own body. Coming back into your body gives you a point of reference where you can feel grounded if at any time you feel too spacey during the exercise.

Chapter Five:
Negativity's Pathway

"The mind is a superb instrument if used rightly...you usually don't use it at all. It uses you. This is the disease."
— Eckhart Tolle[18]

Motion Five: Bring your hands to your heart—right hand on your heart first and then left hand over your right hand. You are preparing to absorb both energies of Mother Earth and the Divine Universe into your heart, but first you must recognize and draw out all negativity. Visualize taking all the negative energy, thoughts, and feelings in both your conscious and subconscious mind into your left hand. This creates a path for all negativity to flow out of your body so that a new pathway to your heart can open.

Throughout the last few motions of the Meditation, we have focused on recognizing, honoring, and welcoming the awareness of the gifts of Mother Earth, as well as the brilliant powers of the Divine Universe. In order to establish a personal link to these energies, reactivate a connection, and open up limitless possibilities for growth and change, we must free our bodies and minds of conscious and unconscious negative beliefs.

The next motion of the Spiral Blueprint Meditation focuses on gathering and releasing all the negative thought patterns trapped in our bodies. To begin, create a pathway for negative thoughts and feelings to leave the body by using the palm of the left hand as it rests against and on top of the right hand. The right hand releases the grounding power of Mother Earth and the all the creative gifts of the universe into the heart center. The left hand will draw out all negativity stored in the wave patterns of our DNA. We claim the power to cast these negative thoughts and feelings out of us forever, creating space for the optimistic and loving messages of the Blue.

Feelings of hopelessness, shame, anxiety, and self-blame that blocked us from experiencing our

---

18 Eckhart Tolle, *The Power of Now: A Guide to Spiritual Enlightenment* (Novato, CA: New World Library, 1999), 58.

connection to the Universal Energy Source are now held in the left hand. Any conditions that limited us from achieving our goals are gone. Recall Dr. Emoto's work with water that we discussed in Chapter One. If a negative thought such as "you disgust me" can have such a profound impact on the molecular structure of water—rendering its crystal pattern chaotic, disorganized, and painful to the eye—and a thought of "peace" can produce perfectly balanced, beautiful crystalline structures, then imagine the impact of our thought patterns on the physiology of our own bodies that contain up to 60 percent water.

Dr. Emoto's work with water crystals powerfully suggests the potential for internal disharmony that may be created by toxic or negative thought patterns. For an even more concrete understanding of this, we have only to look at what hard science tells us about the chemistry of our brains. We know information is communicated within the brain and throughout the body through chemicals called neurotransmitters. These relay signals between nerve cells called neurons. You've probably heard of a few types of neurotransmitters such as serotonin (which affects mood) and dopamine (which helps with depression and focus).

The information transfer between these neurons is responsible for our motivation levels or, in other words, our ability to perform tasks, make healthy decisions, and manifest change in our lives. When our subconscious mind—weighed down by old toxic thought patterns—starts running the show for us, these neurotransmitters begin controlling us, rather than the other way around.

When a negative or hopeless thought becomes habitual, it literally traces itself into the chemistry of the brain and creates a default pathway. It's like cutting across someone's yard every day instead of using the sidewalk. Before long, you've created a dirt path in the grass, and this shortcut is more inviting than going around; without even thinking about it, you take the worn-out path day after day. In the long run, this means new ideas, new possibilities for expressing creativity, and new ways of activating meaningful change in our lives become harder and harder to envision. The brain defaults to the old patterns rather than creating new ones. However, it is possible to change this pattern completely. We simply have to break the cycle.

For many years, I had this beautiful potted rubber plant. At its best, it was nearly four feet high and thick with glossy, dark green leaves. Not long ago, I placed it out on the porch during a sunny afternoon to pick up a few extra rays of sun. Then I quickly moved on to some other task and completely forgot about it. Soon afterward, we had our first full Northeastern-style frost. Lo and behold, when I finally remembered my precious rubber plant, all of its glossy leaves had withered and turned brown. I brought the sad, brown plant back inside and lamented its death to my husband. He took a closer look and noticed that way down near the dirt, between the forked branches of the plant, a new, pale green shoot was struggling to grow. He promptly trimmed off all the dead branches, assuring me the plant would be able to renew itself once it was no longer giving its precious energy to the old, dead leaves. How right he was! Just a few weeks later, several new sprouts emerged along the main trunk and it continued growing back into a thriving, luscious green houseplant.

Our minds and bodies have the same potential of that rubber plant! When we stop giving our energy to the old, useless branches of thought, that energy can be redirected to vibrant new growth. But where do these negative thought patterns begin? Unfortunately, sometimes even one careless comment can affect us for a lifetime. I have a girlfriend who has the sweetest freckles. They make her look ten years younger than she really is, but she hates them. When I say "hate," I mean she can't even talk about them. If there were a medical procedure to have them removed, she would do it. This is all because as a child, an adult said she looked like a speckled calf, innocently teasing her.

If something so simple can change a life so profoundly, what do you think is the long-term effect of continuous and more serious abuse? That is what most of us build up over the course of a lifetime. It is such a shame that this is the case—that careless, cruel or hopeless messages can find their way into our bodies and then affect the way our brains work and the way we see the world. We can grieve the fact that this is so, but there is no reason to believe we cannot change it. We must accept this reality as it is. But within that acceptance is also a vast promise: regardless of the size and depth of your emotional prison, it is in your power to free yourself.

According to Gregg Braden, "When we form heart-centered beliefs within our bodies, in the language of physics, we're creating the electrical and magnetic expression of them as waves of energy, which aren't confined to our hearts or limited by the physical barrier of our skin and bones. So, clearly we're 'speaking' to the world around us in each moment of every day through a language that has no words: the belief-waves of our heart."[19]

If we are indeed speaking to the world at every moment, what is it we are saying? What do we wish to say? Negative, fearful, or hopeless thoughts are physically expressed in terms of electromagnetic waves. We can change the content of these waves, projecting tangible waves of self-acceptance, optimism, possibility, and peace instead. Imagine a world in which all of our vibrations are raised to this degree. What might it look like?

We can trim the withered leaves of the houseplant, creating new pathways for growth and transformation! When I trimmed down all the leaves of my rubber plant, I noticed the new growth did not necessarily follow the patterns of the former growth. The plant began to take on a new and different shape as it grew, one that I couldn't predict but knew would be beautiful in its own way. So, too, can each of our lives take on new shape and beauty—if we only aim our energies in the right

[19] Gregg Braden, The Spontaneous Healing of Belief: Shattering the Paradigm of False Limits, 94.

direction. To begin the process of releasing negativity, we create a pathway from heart to hand. In this step of the Meditation, the left hand is connected to the heart through the right hand, and the palm is open to receive the old negative beliefs—the fears, anxieties, and self-blame. This is the first step toward clearing the energy that surrounds our heart, shifting those "belief-waves" so that they embody our hopes, desires, and positive intentions rather than our fears and limiting beliefs.

I want to acknowledge that this motion in the Spiral Blueprint Meditation has its challenges as well. It can be difficult to release things we have been carrying for a whole lifetime. The more you practice the Meditation, the easier this process will become. It is important to approach all the motions without self-judgment. After all, you are not in a race, and the Meditation will activate your link no matter what; this link is permanent and can never be broken. It only has to be rediscovered.

For some of us, the sensation of drawing out negative thought patterns and old, ingrained beliefs—particularly in the tender area of our hearts—can feel challenging and perhaps even painful. There can definitely be some internal resistance around this process. It may well be the case that some of the negative experiences in your life have had a profound effect on shaping who you are. Perhaps your challenges, struggles, and pain have given you much of your strength. We can honor this truth even as we open ourselves up to releasing the past anxieties and barriers that no longer serve us.

You can perform the following exercise to help you approach this process without blame or judgment, honoring the wisdom of your own body and your own experiences, while at the same time signaling to your heart that you are ready to release the old thought patterns that no longer serve you.

Clear Heart Meditation

This meditation exercise can be performed as often or as rarely as you like. Since it requires that you are in a comfortable, safe space and able to enter a state of deep relaxation, it is best to perform the clear heart meditation when you have at least fifteen minutes to spare and know that you will not be disturbed. Be sure to read through each step of the meditation exercise until you have committed it to memory. Ideally, you want to be able to perform each of the five steps without referring back to the book. Alternatively, you may choose to have a friend or other trusted companion read the steps to you, acting as your guide. If you choose this option, be sure that your guide is someone you completely trust, and have them read in a slow, soothing tone of voice. You might also want to record these steps on a recording device such as your smartphone or tablet and play it back to yourself.

1. Choose a comfortable place where you feel quite safe. If possible, play some relaxing instrumental music in the background while you do the meditation exercise. Make sure the music does not have lyrics that might distract you.

Arrange yourself in a comfortable position, either seated or lying down, so that your whole body feels supported by the surface beneath you.

2. *Begin by relaxing your mind and body with some deep breathing. Inhale deeply and visualize your body being filled with a blue wave of fresh, clean air, all the way from the crown of your head down to your toes. As you slowly exhale, imagine that the blue wave is sweeping any stress or anxiety from your body so that you can release it. Breathe in this way for several moments, allowing your body to relax and feel supported by the surface beneath you. On each inhalation, you are allowing the wave to gather up any tension or discomfort or nagging thoughts. You then release them completely on the exhale, until you reach a place of mental and physical relaxation.*

3. *Once you feel comfortable and relaxed, allow your breath to return to an even, natural rhythm, breathing at whatever pace is comfortable for you. Now, turn your attention to the area of your heart, simply noticing how it feels. Your heart chakra may feel warm and soft and open, or it may feel tense or tight or restricted. However it feels, try to simply notice the feeling without judgment. If it is comforting to you, you may wish to place one or both of your hands over your heart. Just take a moment here to honor how this part of you is feeling, whatever that may be for you in this moment, knowing the feelings here change all the time. Remind yourself that your heart is your oldest friend, it has been with you through thick and thin, and it will always be there for you, no matter what.*

4. *Now, see if you can speak directly to your heart. Either aloud or in your mind, say the following words: "Thank you for being a steady and faithful companion. Thank you for carrying all that you have carried. Now, I am ready to release the things that no longer serve me. Thank you." Make sure you express each word slowly and deliberately. Afterward, simply continue to breathe gently—in and out—noticing whatever comes up without judgment. You may feel a sensation of release or a feeling of resistance, but whatever comes up, there is no need to force anything. Simply notice the feeling. You may repeat the message once or twice if it feels right to do so.*

5. *When you are ready, express a thought of gratitude to your heart, knowing it will always be with you and it can grow and change with you as well. Next,*

inhale deeply to bring yourself out of the clear heart meditation. At your own pace, emerge from your state of relaxation by wiggling your fingers and toes and stretching your muscles. Now, open your eyes. Finally, bring your hands together in a prayer position over your heart. Bowing your head over your hands, express a final "thank you," to your heart, to yourself, to Mother Earth, and to the Divine Universe for being your generous and loving resources.

Chapter Six:
Love, Service, and Gratitude

"You who are the source of all power
Whose rays illuminate the whole world,
Illuminate also my heart
So that it too can do your Work."
— Prayer of Wholeness[20]

Motion Six: Speak the mantra, "Unconditional Universal Love, Unconditional Universal Service, Unconditional Universal Gratitude." As you say these words, keep your hands on your heart and visualize the brilliant white creative light of the Divine Universe and the dense, protective energy of Mother Earth flowing into your heart through your right hand. Concentrate on allowing these energies to fill every cell in your body clearing a path to Unconditional Love, Service, and Gratitude.

In the fourth and fifth motions of the Spiral Blueprint Meditation, we focused on visualizing the grounding resources of Mother Earth and the luminous powers of the unseen Divine Universe, and releasing all negativity stored in the mind and body. In the sixth motion, we open a pathway into our own hearts for both types of energy to be received. The three contact points of the Meditation (you, the Earth, and the Divine Universe) are now integrated. Placing each hand over the heart physically embodies this integration and, by speaking the mantra, "Unconditional Universal Love, Unconditional Universal Service, Unconditional Universal Gratitude," we accept our natural place in the order of the universe. As we awaken to the reality of Universal Unconditional Love, we naturally connect with and express Unconditional Service and Gratitude, for this is our true state. Even though this may feel like heavy and dense territory, it is also as simple as pointing your finger. Think about it. Where do you point your finger when you are referring to yourself? For example, let's say someone asked you, "Who painted that picture?" If you had, would you proudly point to your knee and say,

---

20 Ralph H. Blum, *The Rune Cards: Ancient Wisdom For the New Millennium* (New York, NY: St. Martin's Press, 1989), 155.

"Oh, that painting? I did that." No, of course not. You would point to your heart and say, "I did it."

The HeartMath Institute (HMI), founded in 1991 by Doc Childre, has as its key focus the task of exploring emotions and connections of the heart and mind. The internationally recognized nonprofit organization's research is focused on science-based heart-center studies. According to the HMI Science and Research website:

> *The heart produces by far the body's most powerful rhythmic electromagnetic field, which can be detected several feet away by sensitive instruments. Research shows our heart's field changes distinctly as we experience different emotions. It is registered in people's brains around us and apparently is capable of affecting cells, water and DNA studied in vitro. Growing evidence also suggests energetic interactions involving the heart may underlie intuition and important aspects of human consciousness... The heart and brain maintain a continuous two-way dialogue, each influencing the other's functioning. The signals the heart sends to the brain can influence perception, emotional processing and higher cognitive functions. This system and circuitry is viewed by neurocardiology researchers as a "heart brain.*[21]

We are surrounded by living, pulsing and intelligent energy everywhere; even what we might consider to be solid matter is actually vibrating. According to physics, the vibration or "wave particles," contain information in the vibratory pattern of the object. This information is what makes up our world. We are living in, surrounded by, and made up of wave patterns. These particles continue to hold information from thoughts, actions and/or feelings that exist long after the physical body has forgotten.

What is perceived as the most active body part? And what is the most recognized organ in the body? The brain and *YES* the heart. Hence we have what is referred to as the mind-body connection. What is that connection and what does it mean? The heart is our "gateway," if you will, allowing our physical life experiences (the mind) access to a more spiritual level. In the womb, the heart begins to beat before the brain is formed. When we forget that our heart center is a higher form of brainpower, we allow the body to hold on to unwanted information stored in the body's vibrating particles. According to HMI, our energy pattern can be detected several feet from our bodies. If this is the case, old unwanted experiences, situations, images, and/or feelings trapped within our own DNA could be

---

21 "HeartMath Science and Research," HeartMath Institute, http://www.heartmath.com/research/.

shared with the world around us—The Butterfly Effect strikes again!

The good news is everyone has the ability to clear unwanted stagnant vibrations. We just need to learn how to access the bridge that connects the physical with the higher vibrations where creation is possible. The heart beats to a higher form of intelligence thereby influencing the information process to the brain. Once the heart-mind bridge is established, the heart can communicate with the brain. This information transfer can clear unhealthy perceptions, emotions, and behaviors.

If the heart is the gateway to the mind, how do we gain entrance to our heart center? The higher vibrations of the upper etheric realms always direct an active heart-led mind, also referred to as spirit. This combination can deliver powerful messages of healing, inspiration, empowerment, and love. Gratitude is the gateway to opening the heart center. Once established, the release of negative vibrations starts almost immediately; you feel it and those around you feel it.

So then, what is Unconditional Love? It is the very fabric of the universe—the nonjudgmental, all-loving material that makes up everything around us. It fills in the gaps between all the things you can see and the things you cannot see. Think of it as the glue that holds our cells, our world, and universe together. It is the very material from which you are made. For this reason, it has nothing to do with your actions or what you have experienced in your life up until now. In fact, it separates you from your actions. No matter how much you have been through, how much you may be suffering, or how much guilt you feel, the possibility for reopening your connection with Divine Unconditional Love is always there. There is nothing you can do to make that possibility go away.

Imagine bringing home a brand new puppy. This little creature is still in its learning stages and if it chews up your favorite pair of red sneakers, you would probably still love the puppy. You might feel disappointed about the loss of your most awesome sneakers, but this doesn't make you stop loving the puppy. The puppy is still loveable, even though it has made a mistake. This is how the universe "feels" about *you*. This can be difficult for many of us to accept because most of the love we experience in life is conditional—if we act a certain way, we will be rewarded. If we act another way, we will be punished. This leads to disappointment and feelings of rejection. Often, the love we give ourselves is the most conditional of all, since we tend to be our own most difficult critic.

Self-judgment, guilt, shame, and disappointment with our perceived failures can all build up over the course of a lifetime so that the very idea of Unconditional Love seems strange and unknowable. I assure you, it is not only knowable, it is the surest thing you *can* know. By rediscovering our natural connection to the Earth and the greater universe, we take our rightful place again in the context of Unconditional Love and allow it to fill us up from within. This is our way to wholeness and freedom. We are living now at the end of the Piscean Age, an era in human history characterized by separation rather than unity. The veil of the Piscean Age is dense. It hangs down, dark and heavy, between our eyes and the reality of a loving universe. For the most part, in this Age, we have been denied regular rituals and practices that honor our connection to both Earth and the Divine Universe. There has been no room for lasting heart-based activities in this Age.

Instead, we are encouraged to see ourselves as separate from the Earth and the Divine Universe, and are even encouraged to exploit and dismiss them completely. Success is measured by the accumulation of material objects, without respect to the quality of our relationships with one another or ourselves. Within such a limited view of reality, is it any wonder we feel cut off and isolated from others and our own transcendence? The illusion that we are separate and isolated creates the feeling of being trapped in a gray maze. We become desperate for any avenue that looks like it might have some magic at the end of it. Any substances, activities, and/or emotional discords that are repeated in an addictive way can create the illusion of that magic, which explains why so many of us struggle with such issues.

All human lives have their challenges. I now understand there is an unbreakable link between the fabric that is Unconditional Love and me. When I was a young single mother, my actions, decisions, and opportunities were based in fear; therefore what emerged was fear and disorder. What we focus on, we are. We all have the power to operate from a place of Unconditional Love, Service and Gratitude, which is our authentic center and natural connection to the universe.

The mantra of "Unconditional Universal Love, Unconditional Universal Service and Unconditional Universal Gratitude" is adapted from the teachings of the spiritual healer Zhi Gang Sha. He further describes the intention in his book *The Power of Soul: The Way to Heal, Rejuvenate, Transform and Enlighten All Life*: "Universal service includes universal love, forgiveness, peace, healing, blessing, harmony, and enlightenment....If one offers unconditional service, one receives unlimited blessing."[22]

With Unconditional Universal Love, we attune our bodies to the all-loving Divine Universal Love that created us. We clear away all the negative energy and feelings stored within us associated with the teachings of conditional love. If we fail to love ourselves unconditionally, we will be unable to receive or give love anywhere in life. Speaking the mantra announces your intention to welcome Unconditional Love and to restore your natural connection with the Source. Your hands, holding the love of Mother Earth and the universe, come together and rest over your heart, opening the channel for this energy to flow into your being.

Illuminate Also My Heart

---

22 Zhi Gang Sha, The Power of Soul: The Way to Heal, Rejuvenate, Transform and Enlighten All Life (New York, NY: Atria Books, 2009), 4.

Every individual experiences Love, Service, and Gratitude differently, and the ways in which your connection to these true states plays out in your own life are totally unique. Writing this book and sharing the Spiral Blueprint Meditation is one of the ways Love, Service, and Gratitude have manifested in my life, but you will undoubtedly find you are inspired in other ways.

New creative projects might occur to you, or you may find more healing and forgiveness opening up in your personal relationships. Maybe you will have new ideas about the work you do, or maybe you will discover new business opportunities or financial resources. As you reconnect with the unbreakable loop of Love, Service, and Gratitude, your vibration is raised in such a way that you can attract and draw new possibilities for good things into your life. You begin acting from your truest, deepest self, so that your efforts and actions will emerge naturally from this place.

The prayer, "You who are the source of all power, whose rays illuminate the whole world, illuminate also my heart so that it too can do your Work" is associated with Sowelu, the ancient rune representing the creative, life-giving properties of the sun. [23] In his book *The Rune Cards: Ancient Wisdom for the New Millennium*, Ralph Blum includes a visualization with this prayer that I also suggest as a supplemental exercise. Prayer and mantra are powerful aids to help us focus our minds as we visualize healing and connection. From the place of healing and connection, we bravely begin to manifest our own best, authentic selves. This supplementary visualization and prayer is a good way to welcome healing and creativity into your heart, and also invite the brilliant manifestations that are sure to come once you have done so!

Prayer to the Sun Rune Exercise

1. *Recite the words of the prayer, either out loud or in your mind:*
   - *You who are the source of all power*
   - *Whose rays illuminate the whole world,*
   - *Illuminate also my heart*
   - *So that it too can do your Work.*
2. *As you do so, visualize the light of the sun pouring into your heart, flowing through your body and into the Earth beneath you, then traveling back out*

---

23 Blum, The Rune Cards, 154.

and into the world around you. Repeat the prayer three times if you wish.[24]

From here, Love, Service, and Gratitude emerge naturally. As you begin to act from this place of wholeness and connection, you will naturally be operating at your highest level. Your authentic self can take over, radiating Gratitude and Service from within and rippling out into the world around you in your actions. Love, Service and Gratitude provide a meaningful path, but the meaning of this will be different to each of you. Your path may not look anything like mine, but it will be your right path. By keeping your own channel clear and inviting the light of Unconditional Love into your very being, you create space and the possibility for your own personal manifestations of Service and Gratitude, whatever they may be.

24 Ibid., 155.

Section Three:
Into the Blue

I reach out my hand. Any memory of the thirst and suffering I had just begged to be free from is gone. The miserable, barren landscape and the sad, pitying eyes of the watchers are gone. My lungs are clear and my body no longer feels burned, aching or torn. In the moment I reach out my hand I have no recollection of the dead place at all. I no longer know where I was or how long I was there as all memory of the first experience disappears.

I am now inside a vast space filled with light. It is not exactly a cave and not exactly a tunnel, although its walls are brown and rocky. But it is not linear—there is no beginning and no end. It is more circular and tube-shaped than long and straight.

The place where I am standing perpetually folds in upon itself so that there is no entrance and no exit except the indescribably large openings you can see on the outer part of a cat toy where a cat is able to see and chase a ball. If I walk the tube-like tunnel, I will end up right back where I began as I am certain the large gaping openings encircle the entire structure. I am just a speck, smaller than a grain of sand and look out of the huge, glassless windows that line the outer walls, all of them opening onto a vast stretch of space composed of purest color—Blue.

The shade of blue is difficult to name or describe, but it is so vivid that it seems to contain every possible hue of the color. If you asked me to find a sample swatch of the shade, I could not. It is at once celestial and crystalline and rich and warm. The deep-blue space I am looking into has no horizon and no end. It contains no structures, but it is not empty. Its depths sparkle with millions and millions of orbs of light, all twinkling at various degrees of brightness like stars in a clear night sky—except that they are all moving in the same direction but at various speeds. Some blaze a quick fiery path through the Blue, brilliant as shooting comets. Others move steadily. Still others, dimmer and less clearly visible, drift very slowly. But each makes its way.

I stand and watch this incredibly beautiful display for what seems like hours—or it might be years, centuries, minutes, or seconds. In this place I am outside of time. Time has no meaning. Eventually, I am aware of thinking, "What am I watching?" The moment I have this thought, I am also aware I am not alone. To my right, I feel the presence of three Beings. They are tall and thin, clothed in a whitish-blue aura, and so bright I cannot focus on them directly. I sense kindness from them, and a warmth and friendliness, as though they are old friends. Without speaking, I ask them what the lights are. As I communicate the question, I seem to leave my body and look down into the circular cave from above. From high up, I can see the three Beings and myself. At the same time, I know that I am in my body, standing next to them. Somehow, without language, they speak to me.

They communicate that every single thing that has ever existed is contained within one of the spectacles of luminous lights I now see before me. Our bodies are not what we see in the mirror. We cannot look upon our true selves with human eyes; the light would blind us. The beautiful orbs of radiant glimmering light shimmer with our essential true selves, in the form of pure energy. I am told that each of the lights is on a journey. Each glow is on a very personal course, one of sacred learning and discovery back to the Source. The collective wholeness adds to all that we are an individual part of—the galaxies, the universe, the planet, and ourselves.

The brighter, fast-moving lights clear a path to move toward the Source more quickly here in the material world. This might occur over many lifetimes or one. The slower lights still have material issues to move beyond, or may simply choose to remain where familiarity is steadfast, as they are not ready to move on so fast. I am told some even become too familiar with death, not recognizing yet that there is more beyond that energetic level. Still others have such a strong attachment to earthly concepts—such as sin or judgment of what they considered sin—that they are afraid to move forward thinking they will be judged as they were on Earth. Each is living out an undertaking of learning at an individual pace, but ALL return eventually to the Source.

At that moment, every iniquity, every wrong doing, every hurt, harsh word, or bad thought I ever caused flashes before me. The fact that all or any of us return seems wrong to me and I vaguely think "Hitler?" It is shown to me that our truest nature, our real soul is a balance of precise beauty, love, service, and gratitude. All that is—is perfect. This doesn't make sense to me. In fact, I don't understand much of what is being passed on to me. I am shown a very faint almost immobile orb. I suddenly realize what we are here to learn, share and take with us is that we are perfect. Until a soul realizes this, that soul will not move forward, and sometimes will repeat many lifetimes in order to acquire this knowledge.

The beauty that is spread out before me seems to be nothing compared to the beauty of what I feel in every single cell and particle of my being. I wonder if the luminous lights did not realize their own perfectness without guidance like I was receiving, how would they know to even strive to glimpse the Blue? The Blue holds and supports all the constituents of the physical universe—atoms, plants, ecosystems, people, societies, galaxies—all that is seen and all that is unseen.

I am connected to the energy of the Blue with my entire being in a secure and unbreakable bond. In the same way, the Blue is entangled with each pulsing orb of light. The Blue contains and holds everything without judgment. I occupy all of time and space and yet I am still trying to reason with human beliefs, judging all I see. The Blue has no praise for the more brilliant or fast-moving orbs of light, and it has no blame for the dim or slow-moving ones. The Blue is love—pure and boundless. It is love without conditions, without expectations, without fear, without loss or gain, and without end. It is Divine Unconditional Love and it is everything.

"The Blue is so wonderful," I think. "Beyond wonderful—it is pure joy, safety, beauty, and pure love. Of course some lights want to hang back and stay within it! I want to stay here myself." As I think this, I realize the strangest thing of all— I am already in the Blue and have always been since the dawn of time, and maybe even before.

If I had been someone else having this experience I would be looking out of a different Torus into the Blue, seeing all the luminous lights passing by on their journey, and one of the lights would have my name at this moment in time. I don't know how long I am there until I see the Torus for what it is and myself for what I am—one of the traveling luminous orbs. I wonder how fast and how *bright my light is in the Blue. At last, I see the truth that we are all connected, we are a community of all that is, was and will be, and together we create universes, galaxies, atoms—all that is seen and unseen. We are all one and now it matters to me how brightly I shine within the Blue.*

"What is the Source?" I ask the Beings, who stand by silently and patiently await my next thought. Without words, they show me how to understand the nature of the Source. The Source is like a single, glimmering crystal prism. When light shines through the prism, it creates countless beautiful refracted aspects of its own light. All three are needed: the light, the prism, and all the countless aspects of refracted light are required to make the complete and beautiful whole. This is the Source.

Thus we are all separate and all connected by our own Source energy.

The Source is both our origin and our destination like one big Universal Torus looping in and out of its self. From it, we are born and to it we all return eventually, though for some, the journey may take longer than for others. Still no one ever completely stops moving forward on the way back to the Source. Absolutely everyone returns—it is a never-ending loop.

We are all a necessary part of this greater fabric. If even one single thing were different, there would be a "hole" in the Blue, a missing piece of the puzzle. We are all made up of energy, which can neither be created nor destroyed. It can only be transformed. If we can release our fears, we can take our rightful place within the all-loving Blue, here and now.

Inside the Torus, I am standing within my own light aspect—my true self—my own past, present, and future continually looping around. I am given the chance to see the world from my own torus of energy. This perfect place is the real me, the genuine me. Everyone is connected—we need each other to change and grow. If an individual is healthy, happy and free, so is the Blue. I understand it is my responsibility to bring this knowledge back and release my own butterfly. As soon as I have this realization, a sudden rattling sound snaps me back into my physical body.

I awoke from this experience drenched in sweat. I was lying on the office sofa at the mental health group home where I worked as a counselor on the full-time graveyard shift, one of my three jobs at the time. The home housed twelve residents who were transitioning from long-term rehab back into society. It was a very old home, and at the time, not much funding went into its structural needs. Was the loud rattling that had snapped me back into consciousness just the wind rattling the original old windows and doors? Was it a resident trying to get inside after curfew? Or was it an ex-resident, maybe, back on drugs and with nowhere else to go, rattling the door to be heard? Any one of these scenarios would not have been uncommon, but somehow I knew none of them had been the source of the rattling. Then, even more strangely, I noticed each of the windows of the old house began to rattle, one by one, like a wave around the old home. The sound rippled slowly through the boards of the walls, through each pane of glass, and through every door, one by one. Besides the slow-moving rattle, the only other sound was the crackly, static hum of the television, which had gone off air.

I sat up, confused and now a little more than scared. Could this be an earthquake on the East Coast? *No, not an earthquake*, I thought. *If it was, everything would be shaking at once, instead of in this strange rippling pattern.* Then, as suddenly as the sound began, it stopped. Had I imagined it? I shut off the TV and made my way through the dimly lit office into the dark kitchen and snapped on the light. The sudden brightness of the fluorescent lighting in the kitchen assaulted my eyes. The shaking had stopped completely; all that was left was the silence inside and out. It was the kind of unsettling quiet that can sometimes settle over a small country town in the middle of the night. I felt as if I were the only person in the world.

As I stood in the brightly lit and silent kitchen, my heart was pounding. Then suddenly everything in my visions—before the shaking of the doors and windows—came rushing back to me, and I had to sit down. I looked at the clock. I estimated it could have only been fifteen minutes or less between the time when I did the last check and when the shaking started, yet the experience seemed to have occupied hours, weeks, centuries. The memory came flooding back to me in perfect detail, and I knew with my whole being that the world, for me, was forever changed.

When I finally calmed down from the wave of energy rattling through the old house, the entire voyage was engrained in my mind. It was more real to me than any event I have had in "real life" and I knew I needed to live my life in a different way. This experience was a life-changer. Just like the house shaking had jolted me from sleep, the journey I had taken shook me to my very core. I was now fully awake in more ways than one.

I was given a glimpse of what true Unconditional Love, Service and Gratitude could mean to my life if I actively attempted to live them. At the time, I had no reference point for the experience. I had never heard of out-of-body experiences, and I couldn't even name what had happened in those words. In fact, I still can't really say what it was exactly. All I know is that, within a few seconds, the universe opened up—or my consciousness opened up to it—and I saw the world as it really is, behind the veil.

Nothing has been the same since. All of a sudden I knew, for certain, what today's quantum physicists are saying conclusively: there is no empty space. There is only one, vast, interconnected fabric of energy, and we are beings of light contained within that fabric, bound to it and to one another in an incomprehensibly beautiful network of entanglements. The fabric itself is Unconditional Love. All of my partying and reckless behavior had all been in search of that feeling.

Once I connected with it, the connection could never be broken. The path before me became clear. I could stop questing, questioning, worrying, and torturing myself with self-judgment and fear of the future. I felt so relieved! And as I held onto that feeling, I allowed myself to be guided by it. A whole world of possibility began to open up. I was no longer defined by my ego and fears, but only by what I really believed and wanted to do. I began to see opportunities where none had existed before, and I began walking a path of balance without struggling against it or wondering if I was missing something.

I emerged from the Blue knowing life has a comfort and natural flow it did not have before.

Chapter Seven:
Releasing Negativity

"The world would have you agree with its dismal dream of limitation.
But the light would have you soar like the eagle of your sacred visions."
—Alan Cohen[25]

Motion Seven: Keep your feet in place, and turn to the left as far as is comfortable. As you turn, drop your left hand toward the ground, palm down, and release all known and unknown negativity into Mother Earth where it can be received and cleansed. The action will look and feel like you are slowly throwing what isn't needed anymore out onto the ground behind you. As you prepare to perform the next motion, keep your left palm open and positioned behind you.

In the fifth and sixth motions of the Spiral Blueprint Meditation, we focused on drawing negativity out of the body into the left hand and clearing a path for Unconditional Love, Service, and Gratitude to enter the heart through the right hand. Now, in the seventh motion, we cast all that negativity out of ourselves, releasing it into the ground where the limitless resources of Mother Earth can absorb and process it for us. With this gesture, we express our faith in the healing and restorative powers of the Earth even as we rid ourselves of that which no longer serves us. This gesture is both grounding and clearing. In this motion and the next two motions, we are physically clearing the energetic space that surrounds our bodies, opening up the powerful channel between Mother Earth, the Creating Universe, and ourselves.

The Meditation clears the energetic space that travels through your body and surrounds you, otherwise known as your personal torus. As mentioned before, the torus may be best visualized as a donut shape, or in my case, a cat toy. There is a central core, each end of which is a vortex, so that energy flows into one end, through the center, out the vortex on the other end, and then loops around

25 Dr. Purushothaman, Words of Wisdom (Volume 29): 1001 Quotes & Quotations (Kollam, Kerala, India: Centre for Human Perfection, 2014), 27.

the outside of the sphere until it returns again to the first vortex. The torus energy process exists in many examples from nature, such as tornados or vortexes seen in water, or the observable magnetic fields surrounding planets, stars, and planetary systems. It can be seen in the energetic process of our own blood cells as well as on the quantum level of atoms and subatomic particles. We might even visualize everything that IS as a series of toroidal energy patterns nested within one another like Russian dolls: the Earth's atmosphere a torus within the toroidal heliosphere surrounding the Sun; the organisms of Earth's toroidal systems nested within the planet's atmosphere; the cells within the organisms of each torus nested within the those organisms, and so on.

According to Marshall Lefferts, founder of the Cosmometry Project and former Consulting Producer of the Buckminster Fuller Institute, "the torus is the fundamental form of balanced energy flow found in sustainable systems at all scales. It is the primary component that enables a seamless fractal embedding of energy flow from micro-atomic to macro-galactic wherein each individual entity has its unique identity while also being connected with all else."[26]

To put it simply, in the words of researcher Arthur Young, "The self in a toroidal Universe can be both separate and connected with everything else."[27] As individuals, we each possess our own torus, our own separate dynamic energetic flow pattern. Energy flows in through the head and the feet, then loops out around the body in all directions at about an arm's length, and then reconnects and flows back in through the head and feet. Our personal energy flows through our bodies and then bends back into itself in a continuous cycle. This is why it is so important to keep our personal torus clear, so that we can maintain our open and receptive state to the other contact points of the Meditation. By releasing negativity and limiting beliefs and fears, we refresh and cleanse the energy loop. This allows us to function harmoniously in connection to all the other torus-shaped energy patterns surrounding and interacting with us, including other people, animals, plants, trees, the Earth itself, and the larger universe.

Thinking our own energy has *no* effect on the world around us is like driving a car on a crowded highway as if there were no other cars on the road. Yes, each driver is contained in his or her individual car, but it is only an illusion that makes the drivers separate. We understand as drivers that we are in fact dependent upon one another to drive in the expected way, and safely. When someone messes up, there is an instantaneous and measurable impact on everything surrounding the mistake. This is a concrete way of visualizing what is happening all the time in the matrix of interconnected energies that we are all part of. We are not separate from one another or from the Earth. All is connected on the

---

26 "The Torus - Dynamic Flow Process," Cosmometry Project, http://www.cosmometry.net/the-torus---dynamic-flow-process.
27 Ibid. To read more about Arthur Young, see http://www.arthuryoung.com/index.html.

level of energy, and a growing body of scientific evidence is describing the impact of these energetic connections on the material, visible world.

In his lecture titled "Language of the Divine Matrix" recorded in Italy in 2007, Gregg Braden presented phenomenal video footage from the Huaxia Zhineng Qigong Clinic and Training Center—or "medicine-less hospital"—in Qinhuangdao, China. In the footage, three trained healers are seen practicing on a patient with bladder cancer. As they chant, focusing their personal energies on the belief the patient's cancer *has already been healed,* the tumor visibly disappears in the real-time sonogram image. The practitioners are able to remove the patient's tumor without drugs, radiation, or surgery. The healing happens on the energetic level as the result of *belief,* and then manifests on the material level—in this case, the material transformation of disease.[28]

If a clear personal torus encourages balance and harmony, you can easily imagine the effects of its opposite. When our personal torus is blocked or inhibited by limiting beliefs and fears, equally negative consequences such as depression, hopelessness, feelings of disconnection, and even despair or disease may be the result.

The seventh, eighth, and ninth motions of the Spiral Blueprint Meditation are specifically designed to engage your body as an agent for clearing your personal torus. This is why you keep your left palm pointing downward—palm out and behind you—at the end of this motion and into the next. In doing this, the left hand is linked with the Earth's lower, denser vibrations, where creation takes place. This is both clearing and balancing. Releasing negativity is not something that can be done with the mind alone. In fact, as I have already discussed, much of the negativity we carry is the product of our linear left brain. This part of our mind produces limiting beliefs associated with the past as well as fear of the future. The movements of the Meditation engage your entire body so that your brain can get out of the way.

In practicing all the motions in the Meditation, you gain access to the continual flow of positive energy from which and into which you were born. In this way, you can begin to harmonize your own energy with all the energy systems that surround you. From here, you will experience life in flow, and your ideas and actions will emerge from a place of balance and clear intuition. Clearing and keeping your personal torus flowing properly maximizes harmony and benefits you not only personally, but also benefits the greater fabric of the Earth and the universe as well. It is possible to become harmoniously aligned with the Earth, its inhabitants, and the etheric dimensions that are not visible to the naked eye. When we practice this, our greatest gifts and most generous wishes for others can actually become our reality.

---

28 Gregg Braden, Language of the Divine Matrix, DVD, edited by Claudio Corvino, (New World Multimedia, 2010).

Perhaps the core negative emotion we struggle with is fear, for fear is often the underlying cause of our other hopeless or anxious feelings. Fear of failure can keep us from pursuing our most authentic dreams, from achieving all that we have the potential to achieve. Fear is the ultimate limiting belief. The fear of death, in particular, lurks beneath the surface of things for many of us, whether acknowledged or not. Mistakenly, we may fear that death represents a terrifying end—that it is the end of us.

My experience demonstrated to me that death is not like the period that closes the sentence, or the end. Energy can neither be created nor destroyed. We are energy. We can only transform. There is nothing to fear, and once we realize that, we realize that we have no limitations. We are surrounded by limitless love and possibility; if we let go of our fear, we can begin to participate in that. We become centered, in flow with the energies that surround us, and capable of more than we ever dreamed possible. We can, as the words of Alan Cohen at the beginning of this chapter suggest, transcend a "dismal dream of limitation" and "soar like the eagle of our sacred visions."

Releasing Fear Meditation

One of the most common negative feelings we tend to hold is the emotion of fear. We fear the future, we fear our failures, and we fear death. Releasing fear is an important part of keeping your personal torus clear. The following meditation exercise is from Brad Austen, an intuitive meditation teacher trained in Psychic Development and Mediumship, and can be found on YouTube.[29] This exercise is simple and can be practiced virtually anytime, anywhere. Use it as a supplementary meditation exercise to help you practice releasing the primary negative emotion of fear.

1. *Begin by calling on the light, Archangel Michael, God or whatever you perceive it to be. Take a deep breath in and exhale gently.*
2. *Become aware of the speed of your breathing. By breathing deeply and slowly, your body and mind gradually relax.*
3. *Take another deep breath in and exhale gently.*

Visualize a violet transmuting laser of light coming down into your crown at the top of your head. See this laser zapping away any negativity, any fear-based energies. This violet laser of light is transmuting any fear-based energy that may be affecting you now.

---

[29] Brad Austen, "Releasing Fear Meditation (Guided Meditation)," March 28, 2015, https://www.youtube.com/watch?v=HdFGGjxzyOo.

4. *Keep calling on the light to transmute your fears now, whatever they may be. Fear can manifest in different ways: phobias, fears or repetitive habits. See this violet light transmuting your fears and returning them to neutral energy. Within a few minutes, your fear or anxiety will reduce and become more manageable.*

5. *Ask the light to seal your aura and visualize your aura becoming clear and strong.*

6. *If you are still feeling some fear at this point, visualize the fear-based energies bouncing off your aura. This energy can no longer penetrate your aura and body.*

7. *Ask the light to take away any energy or entities not for your highest good.*

8. *Ask the light to remove these energies from you on a full and permanent basis now.*

9. *Finally, visualize the violet light sealing your aura with light and protection, so that only love-based energies may enter your field.*

10. *If you can, try to hold a happy or joy-filled emotion in your heart.*

11. *Allow this feeling to expand out from your heart and expand throughout your entire body and aura.*

12. *Thank the light for helping you during your time of need.*

13. *Remember that we have free will. Spirit respects our free will, and so we need to ask for assistance when required.*

Whenever you feel anxious or fearful, remember to practice this meditation. Over time, your fears will lessen and become more manageable, but it does require effort and practice.

Chapter Eight:
Receiving

"The intellect has little to do on the road to discovery.
There comes a leap in consciousness, call it intuition or what you will,
and the solution comes to you and you don't know how or why."
— Albert Einstein[30]

Motion Eight: While your left hand stays open behind you, gently readjust your left hand, but keep it open and slowly turn your upper body to the right as far as is comfortable for you. Think of it as a flowing Tai Chi movement. As you turn to the right, reach your right hand up towards the sky like you are picking an apple off a tree from a ladder and the apple is behind you. Your right hand is now cupped, palm up, and ready to accept all the positive healing energy of the Universe.

Visualize pure white light falling like a warm, wonderful shower, as you soak pure love and healing energy deep into every cell in your body. Imagine a warm blanket of protection coming up from the Earth and completely surrounding you with refreshing, beautiful and creative energy. Let that energy flow into your right hand, through your body, and then down towards Mother Earth through your left hand. Repeat the same meditative motions using your opposite side.

At the end of each repetition visualize an explosion of pure white, loving light bursting forth from you in all directions, out into the Universe, surrounding and covering the Earth. Like the twist in your DNA and the loop of your personal torus, you have created and aligned yourself with the pure energy of Unconditional Universal Love, Unconditional Universal Service, and Unconditional Universal Gratitude.

---

30 For more quotes from Albert Einstein, see https://www.entheos.com/quotes/by_topic/Albert+Einstein.

In this next-to-last motion of the Spiral Blueprint Meditation, we open ourselves up fully to receive the phenomenal gift that is our connection to both Mother Earth and the Divine Universe itself. The raised right hand welcomes the creative and healing energies of both these contact points, which then traverse the personal torus and continue the energetic cycle back down into the Earth.

The previous motions of the Meditation have released negativity and cleared the torus, so the energy is now free to flow—unfettered—along its natural path. From this place of alignment, we experience the permanent, unbreakable link between our unique personal energy and the greater fabric to which we are joined. The visualization at the end of this chapter allows us to see our energy in harmony with all else, a reality that spreads light, healing, and power from our own personal center out into the rest of the world and the universe. Your personal torus is your connection to the Earth and to the etheric plane. It is the articulation of your presence in the divine grid and your personal refraction of light shining through the prism that is the Blue. When it is clear and aligned, it spins in synchronicity with the Earth's rotations. This synchronicity of spin aligns with the Creating Universe, granting us the ability to manifest positive transformations both personally and globally.

Visualizing these energetic connections and knowing they are real may come more easily to some people than others. For some, a personal experience may have already granted a glimpse behind the veil. For others, there is simply a natural logic to the idea that, as beings of energy, we are connected to and constantly interacting with a larger energetic pattern. For still others, these ideas may feel more abstract and more difficult to wrap the mind around.

Whatever the case, you may be familiar with the idea of "coming from the gut," or operating from a place of instinct that is located, literally, in one's "gut" or gravitational center. We commonly understand this as the location of our intuition or instinct. Even if blankets of energy and showers of light sound too ethereal, most of us know—like Einstein's quote at the beginning of this chapter—that the intellect alone is not solely responsible for our greatest insights or moments of inspiration. There is another kind of knowing that we connect with in the "gut."

Taking your rightful place—of wholeness, balance, and right action—within the universal energy grid requires that you trust your own deepest knowing, and connect with the gut-center of your power. In Asian energy arts such as Tai Chi and Aikido, as well as chakra mapping systems associated with the practice of yoga, this central point of personal power is *both* an energetic location *and* a physical location. Depending upon which mapping system is used, this point is identified just above the naval or just below it. It may be called the "one point," *tan tien,* the third chakra, or power chakra. It is also the central point of your personal torus.

As Marshall Lefferts of the Cosmometry Institute explains, "It is the still-point singularity that connects our *physical-energetic* being with the entirety of the universe, into the Unified Field itself."[31] To be in touch with and to act from this place is to come from your own unique place of personal power.

In Western culture, the concept of "power" is often confused with ideas of control or dominance. This is not the kind of power I am talking about. Each of us has our own wellspring of personal power: the potential to act, to create, to transform. If we fail to connect with our authentic power, we may experience imbalance in a variety of ways. We may become overly passive, believing our opinions do not matter or that we have no ability to change our lives. On the other hand, imbalance in the power center can also lead to overly controlling behavior, where we try to exert too much control over ourselves or others and become highly self-critical or domineering. As in all things, there is a healthy balance that we each have the potential to reach and to maintain.

When there is a healthy balance—acceptance of personal power combined with acceptance of what we cannot control—we become the most free to realize our ambitions harmoniously, without detriment to ourselves or others. We feel motivated and engaged with life, without needing to exercise too much control over it. The Serenity Prayer, which you might have heard at one time or another, provides an eloquent expression of this state: *God grant me the serenity to accept the things I cannot change, the courage to change the things I can, and the wisdom to know the difference.* Whether you identify with God as an outside entity or a higher power or not, the wisdom of these words is clear. Connection with your power chakra can grant you this same serenity, courage, and wisdom.

When we connect with this central point of our personal power and maintain it in a clear and healthy state, we are better able to access our intuition—that deep and highly personal source of wisdom that goes beyond the often distracting chatter of our intellectual mind. From our intuitive center, we can be capable of what Einstein describes as "a leap in consciousness." In other words, we know exactly what to do or how to manifest what it is we want to see in our world. We are inspired. So often, we think of the universe as a hostile place. Our personal lives might be filled with stress and anxiety; the world around us may appear hopelessly damaged and suffering. We may really feel as if we have lost the power to change our own lives or affect the greater problems of the world. Nothing could be further from the truth. We are each born with transformative power, and it resides here on this Earth and within our very bodies. The connection that takes place when the torus is clear and grounded to Mother Earth, as well as connected with the etheric realms, gives us a window into the state of divine wonder that truly surrounds us. We can open ourselves to receive this ever-present gift.

In the final motions of the Spiral Blueprint Meditation, we experience our link to all that is—in a way that can never be undone—as the radiant, interconnected web that it is. Here, the three contact

---

31 "The Human Experience," Cosmometry Project, http://www.cosmometry.net/human-experience.

points of the Meditation—you, the Earth, and the Divine Universe—are integrated, re-opening the permanent loop that exists among them. Your raised right hand links to the vibrations of the upper realms, where you manifest and take your place within the universal truth of Love, Service, and Gratitude. How and when you experience this connection is up to you, and there is no way for you to do this wrong. You may perceive the connection while practicing the Spiral Blueprint Meditation or in random moments throughout the day where you are granted a momentary window, a glimpse behind the veil. But it can also be experienced every moment of every day. How this happens is up to you, and however it happens is okay. When we reclaim and balance our own personal power and connection, we grow toward a life that is engaged, joyful, healthy, and beautiful. From here, we recognize life itself as the gift it is. In turn, we naturally express our own greatest gifts and participate in our world for the better, both personally and globally.

Connecting With Your Power

This supplementary exercise is designed to bring awareness to your own personal power chakra, or the energetic center of the personal torus. In keeping the power chakra clear and grounding your actions from this place, you can accept your own individual power within the larger framework of the universe.

When you come from a place of balance within yourself and everything else, you can do no harm. Instead, you radiate positivity and creative possibility from your very center. At the same time, you attract those same gifts back to yourself. Such is the natural order of the universe.

Some chakra systems locate the power chakra or the third chakra in the solar plexus, slightly above the naval; others identify it as a point just below the naval. See if one or the other of these locations feels more accurate to you personally. If you do not have a strong feeling either way, choose one of the two locations to focus on and keep that as the focal point for the following meditation exercise.

Power Chakra Meditation

1. *To begin, find a comfortable position, either seated or standing, where you can feel your feet in contact with the ground. It is important to feel grounded for this meditation exercise, so if possible, avoid a reclined or cross-legged position. Consciously bring your awareness to your feet or to your lower body, taking a moment to be aware of your solid connection to the Earth.*
2. *Now, practice a simple cleansing breath cycle: inhale deeply as you count to*

four; hold the in-breath for the counts of five and six; then exhale completely and hold the breath out for counts seven and eight. Repeat this cycle several times for two minutes or so, focusing on the breath and allowing your body to relax and your mind to become clear of other concerns.

3. *Allow your breath to return to a natural, comfortable rhythm. Bring your awareness to your third chakra. Take a moment to simply notice, without judgment, how this area feels right now. A color may appear to you as well. Simply take note of the color, without judgment. Accept whatever comes up. If it feels right to do so, you may place one or both of your hands over the power chakra.*

4. *Now, see if you can visualize your power chakra becoming a warm shade of orange, deep yellow or orange-red. Think of the warmth of the sun on a clear summer day. Visualize the color of such a sun and see if you can bring that warmth into your power chakra.*

5. *Either aloud or in your mind, repeat the following mantra: "This is mine. This is my power. I am in my power, and I am grateful."*

6. *Now imagine a radiant light, red or orange or deep yellow, streaming forward from this place and suffusing your entire body.*

7. *Visualize the streaming rays of light coming gradually back down into your third chakra, until they are contained once more as a gently glowing orb of light.*

8. *Breathe in deeply once more and gradually exhale. Slowly open your eyes and bring your awareness back into the world around you.*

Throughout your day, you can periodically bring your awareness back to that glowing orb of light at your third chakra and see if you can imagine yourself acting from this place. Whenever you do this, also take a moment to feel your feet on the ground or to feel the connection between your lower body (below the power chakra) and the Earth. Some chakra systems locate the power chakra or the third chakra in the solar plexus, slightly above the naval; others identify it as a point just below the naval. See if one or the other of these locations feels more accurate to you personally. If you do not have a strong feeling either way, choose one of the two locations to focus on and keep that as the focal point for the following meditation exercise.

Power Chakra Meditation

1. *To begin, find a comfortable position, either seated or standing, where you can feel your feet in contact with the ground. It is important to feel grounded for this meditation exercise, so if possible, avoid a reclined or cross-legged position. Consciously bring your awareness to your feet or to your lower body, taking a moment to be aware of your solid connection to the Earth.*

2. *Now, practice a simple cleansing breath cycle: inhale deeply as you count to four; hold the in-breath for the counts of five and six; then exhale completely and hold the breath out for counts seven and eight. Repeat this cycle several times for two minutes or so, focusing on the breath and allowing your body to relax and your mind to become clear of other concerns.*

3. *Allow your breath to return to a natural, comfortable rhythm. Bring your awareness to your third chakra. Take a moment to simply notice, without judgment, how this area feels right now. A color may appear to you as well. Simply take note of the color, without judgment. Accept whatever comes up. If it feels right to do so, you may place one or both of your hands over the power chakra.*

4. *Now, see if you can visualize your power chakra becoming a warm shade of orange, deep yellow or orange-red. Think of the warmth of the sun on a clear summer day. Visualize the color of such a sun and see if you can bring that warmth into your power chakra.*

5. *Either aloud or in your mind, repeat the following mantra: "This is mine. This is my power. I am in my power, and I am grateful."*

6. *Now imagine a radiant light, red or orange or deep yellow, streaming forward from this place and suffusing your entire body.*

7. *Visualize the streaming rays of light coming gradually back down into your third chakra, until they are contained once more as a gently glowing orb of light.*

8. *Breathe in deeply once more and gradually exhale. Slowly open your eyes and bring your awareness back into the world around you.*

Throughout your day, you can periodically bring your awareness back to that glowing orb of light at your third chakra and see if you can imagine yourself acting from this place. Whenever you do this, also take a moment to feel your feet on the ground or to feel the connection between your lower body (below the power chakra) and the Earth.

Chapter Nine:
Getting to the Heart of it All

"Your vision will become clear only when you can look into your own heart.
Who looks outside, dreams; who looks inside, awakes."
— Carl Jung[32]

__Motion Nine:__ Slowly turn and face forward. All in one movement, bring your right hand to your heart. Bring your left hand up to cover your right hand. Tap your heart three times. Repeat on the opposite side.

We are energy. We are beings of light connected to a vast fabric of light. We are also human beings, that is, spirits contained within bodies. On the journey to healing, wholeness, and the full realization of the unique gifts we have been tasked to bring into this world, we must accept with gratitude and ultimately embrace our presence within our bodies. As embodied beings, we often experience pain and suffering, yes. However, this state is also a great gift, because it enables us to participate in the beautiful mystery that is life through the medium of our fragile but powerful and remarkable earthly bodies. In this final motion of the Meditation, we connect with the heart, the physical location of our greatest wisdom and our most powerful avenue for connection, healing, and the transformation of our reality as human beings on the Earth.

The heart is the physical location where love is experienced. Past injuries to the heart—old hurts, lack of connection, or heartbreak—tend to result in our closing off the heart, perhaps believing this is the only way to protect ourselves. When we build barriers around the heart, we keep Universal Unconditional Love from flowing, both in and out. In the ninth motion of the Meditation, tapping your heart is a way of expressing gratitude to yourself for your capacity to connect with love, and opening the heart to receive the Divine Unconditional Love that is your birthright. At the same time, it is a physical cue reminding you that the universe itself is composed of Unconditional Love and you, personally, are a unique, embodied particle of that infinite fabric from which you came, in which you

32 For more quotes from Carl Jung, see http://www.brainyquote.com/quotes/quotes/c/carljung146686.html.

live, and to which you will inevitably return. Tapping your heart can be used as a simple reminder of this any time you wish as you move through your day.

Chapter Eight talked about the physical-energetic location known in Tai Chi as *tan tien*, also called the power chakra according to yogic tradition. Tai Chi and other energy arts place great importance on two other physical-energetic centers of knowledge as well, which are located in the chest and the center of the forehead: the heart chakra and third-eye chakra. Taken together, these three points may also be called the Hara Line. When all three are in harmony, our actions, decisions, and interactions with others are in flow.

The HeartMath Institute describes this state as "coherence."[33] According to HMI, coherence takes place when the mind and heart are aligned and working together. This allows us to override those tricky ego-based decision making processes and access the much more profound wisdom of our intuitive heart center. Because the heart actually emits electromagnetic waves, the state of coherence translates, in a practical sense, into increased personal peace and balance, as well as improves how we function with others. The impact is personal, professional, social, and global.

In an interview, Gregg Braden shared a piece of wisdom he gained in conversation with the abbot of a Buddhist monastery in Tibet. Braden asked the monk what force holds the universe together, and the abbot replied through a translator, "compassion." Somewhat confused, Braden asked for clarification, wanting to understand whether compassion is a feeling we experience or a force. The abbot replied that it is both.[34] As I read this, I felt an incredible thrill of recognition. From my own experience, I understand that compassion is indeed both. When I connected with the Blue, I saw that compassion, or what I think of as Universal Unconditional Love, is the thing that binds everything together.

For some time now, scientists have understood there is no empty space in the universe. With telescopes such as the Chandra X-Ray Space Observatory, we can actually see a network of energy filling up space that was once believed to be empty. I believe that energy is love or compassion. According to Gregg Braden, "It is the compassion in our hearts that creates the waves (the belief waves of electrical and magnetic energy) that align us with this field."[35] Because we have compassion in our hearts, we hold the most powerful energetic potential of the universe within ourselves; it is within our very bodies. In our culture, we often tend to confuse compassion with sympathy or pity—feeling sorry

[33] "The Energetic Heart is Unfolding," July 22, 2010, The HeartMath Institute, https://www.heartmath.org/articles-of-the-heart/science-of-the-heart/the-energetic-heart-is-unfolding/.
[34] "Gregg Braden on Living in the Heart, Beauty, Compassion, Healing, the Master Plan, and more," Conscious Life News, August 5, 2012, http://consciouslifenews.com/gregg-braden-living-heart-beauty-compassion-healing-master-plan-video-plus-transcript/1125953/.
[35] Ibid

for others—but this is not the true meaning. The true meaning of compassion is that it gives us the ability to live and act as part of a greater whole—of humanity, the Earth, and the Divine Universe. Acting from this place teaches us what to do for others and for ourselves.

It is no coincidence that, overwhelmingly, individuals who have near-death experiences return to their lives profoundly changed and imbued with a greater sense of compassion. In fact, the most often repeated concept shared from near-death-experiencer retreats is that love, forgiveness, and compassion are the fabric of the universe.[36] My experience revealed to me the truth of Unconditional Love. And since that time, I have strived in my life to demonstrate the natural emergence of Service and Gratitude from that place.

The power we have as individuals to create our reality *from the heart* is something I believe we have always understood. If we look to civilizations of the past or ancient traditions, we find this belief expressed everywhere. According to a proverb of the Cheyenne Native Americans, "Our first teacher is our own heart."[37]

A growing body of scientific evidence suggests this type of understanding is not simply spiritual, but can actually be quantified in physical terms. For a long time, we have known the electromagnetic impulses of the Earth affect our bodies; now, we are beginning to see this effect goes both ways. The electromagnetic impulses emanating from our bodies, particularly from our hearts, affect the Earth as well. Heart-based wisdom can lead us in the direction of peace. It can reveal to us the innovative solutions we need now to improve the quality of life all over the globe. As we move forward to the next stage of our evolution, let us recall and carry this wisdom. Let the heart be our first and most vocal teacher.

In *The Demon-Haunted World: Science as a Candle in the Dark*, Carl Sagan provides the lovely insight that "science is not only compatible with spirituality; it is a profound source of spirituality."[38] Both science and spirituality provide necessary, important means for understanding our universe and the nature of this life we are given. The points of intersection between the two are growing every day, and it is at these intersections that we find a powerful truth: the potential to transform our world for the better lies within each of us.

As you have moved through the Spiral Blueprint Meditation, the energetic space of your torus has been cleared and freed from ego-based negativity. The same is true of the physical-energetic points that make up the Hara Line. Now you are tapping into the permanent loop that already exists between you

---

36 To read some of these near-death experiences, see www.NearDeathExperiencers.wmthost.com.
37 For more Native American Cheyenne proverbs, see http://www.inspirationalstories.com/proverbs/native-american-cheyenne-our-first-teacher-is-our-own-heart/.
38 Carl Sagan, Demon-Haunted World: Science as a Candle in the Dark (New York, NY: Ballantine Books, 1996), 29.

(both your physical self and energetic self) and everything else. In this final motion of the Meditation, you take a moment to acknowledge the center of your greatest power and knowing: the heart. In this lifetime, your heart is the emotional and spiritual center of yourself as an embodied human being. With the gesture of covering your heart with both hands and tapping it three times, you have raised your own vibration from the heart, so that you are humming in tune with the divine miracle of Unconditional Love and compassion—the very stuff of the universe.

Connecting With Compassion

The end of Chapter Five details a supplementary exercise called the clear heart meditation, which is designed to help you release trapped feelings of negativity, limiting beliefs, and old hurts carried within the heart. This is not an easy process, and it is something that should be approached with patience and as little self-judgment as possible. Compassion for yourself and your own process is just as important as compassion for others.

In fact, self-love and self-acceptance help us tap into the experience of Universal Unconditional Love. From there, we naturally begin to feel greater compassion for and connection with others.

In the following exercise, you have the opportunity to visualize the compassion that radiates from your own heart center and out into the world around you. Notice the focus is not to visualize *new* compassion radiating from your own heart center, but instead to visualize the compassion *already* radiating from your own heart center. The compassion is already there—you were born with it. The compassion visualization does not ask you to imagine or create anything; it asks you simply to experience what *is*. This is an extension of the clear heart meditation from Chapter Five and may be practiced as an immediate follow-up as the two move seamlessly into one another. Or you can practice the compassion visualization by itself.

Compassion Visualization

1. Begin by finding a comfortable position. You can practice this seated, standing, or lying down, whatever feels most comfortable to you.
2. Take a moment to attune to your breath, breathing in deeply and evenly, and exhaling slowly and evenly. As you inhale, gather up any tension in your body, and release it on the exhale. After a few cycles, allow your breath to return to

a natural, even rhythm.

3. *Next, turn your attention to your heart chakra. First, simply notice if there are any particular feelings or even colors that come to you as you do so. Honor whatever you notice, without judgment, while continuing to breathe easily and naturally.*

4. *Now, visualize a warm, golden light filling your heart chakra. Imagine the light is literally compassion itself. Allow the light to flow outward from your heart, radiating like the rays of the sun. Allow this radiance to flow throughout your entire body, to the top of your head, and to the tips of your fingers and toes.*

5. *Imagine the golden rays streaming outward from your body, all around you and out into the Universe. Visualize the light flowing further and further out, up, and down into the Earth beneath you, connecting everything in an endless, shimmering web of compassion.*

6. *Finally, place your hands in prayer position over the center of your chest and bow your head slightly. Either aloud or in your mind, repeat the following mantra: "Compassion, always and everywhere, for myself, and all that is."*

7. *When you are ready, slowly open your eyes and ease your awareness back into the world around you.*

Chapter Ten:
Spiral Blueprint Meditation

"There is a vitality, a life force, an energy, a quickening that is translated
through you into action, and because there is only one of you in all time, this expression is unique.
And if you block it, it will never exist through any other medium and it will be lost.
The world will not have it. It is not your business to determine how good it is
or how valuable nor how it compares with other expressions.
It is your business to keep it yours clearly and directly, to keep the channel open."
— Martha Graham[39]

Martha Graham, the mother of modern dance, speaks beautifully of the fact that each one of our souls is wired into a greater fabric that does not judge. As human beings on this planet, our task is not to pass our time in doubt, self-judgment or passivity, but to find a way to "keep the channel open." As a passionately creative dancer and choreographer, Martha Graham understood on a deep level that the physical body is the container for the spirit. Through the body, we can experience the direct link between our truest selves and all that is—the grounding Earth and the Divine Universe.

After the life-changing encounter with the Blue that connected me with the greater fabric of Unconditional Love, I knew I must find a way to maintain my connection with what I had experienced. The Spiral Blueprint Meditation was developed out of my need for a practice that incorporated mind, body, and spirit, and could also be performed easily and in a very short matter of time.

Our lives can unfortunately become limited by toxic beliefs and negative energy patterns trapped in the cells of our bodies and minds. When this happens, our unique, individual expression becomes ensnared and it can be a great struggle to find the way forward. But we can free ourselves. We can connect with the boundless and loving light energy all around us that also emanates from our very bodies. By keeping the channel open, we invite greater abundance, health, joy, and purpose into our lives. We give ourselves the opportunity to live fully.

The Spiral Blueprint Meditation is a simple series of motions or movements that reopen your

---

[39] For more quotes from Martha Graham, see http://en.wikiquote.org/wiki/Martha_Graham.

personal channel to the Divine Universal Energy. The motions—coupled with a simple, sincere intention to be present in the Meditation—can be transformative as they clear your personal energy field and raise your vibration. I believe that in doing the Meditation, you also kick off a spiral of healing and transformation into the world around you.

As a symbol, the spiral matrix represents transformation and evolution. As we stand on the cusp of a new Age, I believe we are being invited to enter the next phase of our own evolution and embrace the potential that lies within the spiral strands of our very DNA.

In practical terms, the Spiral Blueprint Meditation links you with your potential on this plane of reality. It keeps the channel open so your own essential voice can enter the world, allowing you to embody and express all that you were meant to.

The Complete Spiral Blueprint Meditation

It is time to release negative energy and fill your heart with pure Unconditional Love. It is time to clear a path to your soul's intention by entangling it with the powerful healing energy of Mother Earth and the even more infinite and powerful energy of the Divine Universe.

Getting your cells firing together with these powerful energies requires daily repetition of the Meditation for a short period of time. You are simply elevating your positive vibration and displacing negative energy. In doing this, you are creating a new routine for your mind and body, and a new positive pathway for your thoughts to travel. Like any habit, it may begin as a chore, but it is so well worth it. Everyone who has tried the Spiral Blueprint Meditation has reported feeling at least a clearing of their thoughts, if not a powerful shift in awareness and the possibility of a new direction.

The Spiral Blueprint Meditation will likely become a source of comfort, hope, and peace for you. This movement is meant to be repeated frequently, so it is simple and practical by design. The more flexible it is, the more you will use it.

I recommend practicing the exercise for nine days in a row—no less—to start. You will notice the Meditation itself consists of nine motions. This is because of the inherently grounding and magical qualities of the number three. Another trinity you can focus on is that of the universe, the Earth, and you. With the Spiral Blueprint Meditation, your goal is to rediscover the strong connection between these three contact points. You are also creating a positive new habit to replace any negative or toxic belief patterns in your brain. As you continue to practice the Meditation, three (or any multiple of three) repetitions over a chosen period of time will do. Making the exercise your own is more important than following rules.

The first nine days are what I call the activation period. This quickens the alignment and sets it into place. However, you can tailor this to suit you. If you choose to practice the Meditation three times a day for three days, for example, and then take a break, the activation period may simply take a bit longer, but it will happen anyway. There is absolutely no way to do it wrong.

To begin with, I ask that you create an intention. This might be something as simple as "I am loved" or "The change is within me." Feel free to use one of these or come up with your own simple intention. Just go with whatever is in your heart.

Take a moment to focus on your intention. As you do so, imagine that you are connecting your energy with the energy of the universe and grounding your energy in the Earth. Remember, you are creating the foundation for many other intentions in this Meditation.

Now, perform the following nine motions of the Spiral Blueprint Meditation in continuous movement:

> (**Note**: As in Tai Chi, fluidity of movement is more important than exact steps. Be mindful of your movements, but do not worry about doing them perfectly.)

> 1. Stand with your feet shoulder-width apart, knees slightly bent, back straight, and arms at your side. If needed, you may sit in a chair with your back straight and arms resting at your sides or on your lap. Even if you are completely immobile, you can imagine the steps in your mind's eye. The effects will be the same. Your intention is to be in the present moment, in mind and body. Relaxing your mind and body, become aware of how you feel and of your surroundings. Become aware of your breathing in...and out.

> 2. Relax by taking three deep breaths, inhaling deeply and exhaling slowly. With each exhale, relax your body from head to toe. If necessary, keep taking slow deep breaths a little longer than three times. Just breathe in and out until you are fully relaxed, jaw and shoulders soft, and all tension is released throughout your entire body. As you breathe, slowly become aware of the sounds around you. Notice the smells. Become mindful of how you physically feel: peaceful and energized or in pain and tired. Simply become aware—without judgment—of the environment and how your body feels in this moment, but don't think about the connections you have to these things. Relax and allow yourself to simply be aware. If you feel yourself starting to think, judge or worry, return your attention to your breathing. Focusing on even one breath can help you to become mindful again.

> 3. Bring your hands up slowly from the sides of your body, cupping your palms

up in front of you, with elbows slightly bent. Visualize pulling up two handfuls of the energy of Mother Earth, the way you would scoop up a draught of water in your cupped palms. Hold the energy out and up slightly as an offering. As you make this gesture, imagine you are pulling from deep within Mother Earth all her strength, calmness and restorative energy. Give thanks for her gifts.

4. While you are holding your cupped hands up, offer the gifts of Mother Earth and your gratitude to the Universe. Visualize brilliant colors—red, orange, yellow, green, blue, and purple flowing into your cupped hands from the creative center of the galaxy. Once your cupped hands are filled to overflowing, the intense colors transform into a luminous white light that overflows, like a waterfall from your hands. Both the energies—the energy from Mother Earth and the brilliant creative energy of the Divine Universe—mix and fall back to Mother Earth through their most powerful conductor: you. Give thanks to the Universe for this energy.

5. Bring your hands to your heart—right hand on your heart first and then left hand over your right hand. You are preparing to absorb both energies of Mother Earth and the Divine Universe into your heart, but first you must recognize and draw out all negativity. Visualize taking all the negative energy, thoughts, and feelings in both your conscious and subconscious mind into your left hand. This creates a path for all negativity to flow out of your body so that a new pathway to your heart can open.

6. Speak the mantra, "Unconditional Universal Love, Unconditional Universal Service, Unconditional Universal Gratitude." As you say these words, keep your hands on your heart and visualize the brilliant white creative light of the Divine Universe and the dense, protective energy of Mother Earth flowing into your heart through your right hand. Concentrate on allowing these energies to fill every cell in your body clearing a path to Unconditional Love, Service, and Gratitude.

7. Keep your feet in place, and turn to the left as far as is comfortable. As you turn, drop your left hand toward the ground—palm down—and release all known and unknown negativity into Mother Earth where it can be received and cleansed. The action will look and feel like you are slowly throwing what isn't needed anymore out onto the ground behind you. As you prepare to

perform the next motion, keep your left palm open and positioned behind you.

8. *While your left hand stays open behind you, gently readjust your left hand, but keep it open and slowly turn your upper body to the right as far as is comfortable for you. Think of it as a flowing Tai Chi movement. As you turn to the right, reach your right hand up toward the sky like you are picking an apple off a tree from a ladder and the apple is behind you. Your right hand is now cupped, palm up, and ready to accept all the positive healing energy of the Universe.*

9. *Visualize pure white light falling like a warm, wonderful shower, as you soak pure love and healing energy deep into every cell in your body. Imagine a warm blanket of protection coming up from the Earth and completely surrounding you with refreshing, beautiful and creative energy. Let that energy flow into your right hand, through your body, and then down toward Mother Earth through your left hand. Repeat the same meditative motions using your opposite side.*

10. *At the end of each repetition, visualize an explosion of pure white, loving light bursting forth from you in all directions, out into the Universe, surrounding and covering the Earth. Like the twist in your DNA and the loop of your personal torus, you have created and aligned yourself with the pure energy of Unconditional Universal Love, Unconditional Universal Service, and Unconditional Universal Gratitude.*

11. *Slowly turn and face forward. All in one movement, bring your right hand to your heart. Bring your left hand up to cover your right hand. Tap your heart three times. Repeat on the opposite side.*

Afterword:

Let the Spiral Blueprint Begin

Shortly before his death in 1977, the renowned American anthropologist, naturalist, author, philosopher, and educator Loren Eiseley received an award from the U.S. Humane Society for his significant lifetime contributions to "the improvement of life and environment in this country."[40] Eiseley was a thinker of diverse capabilities who fused science with poetry and objective observation with a spirit of wonder and compassion. His 1969 essay, "The Star Thrower" contains a story that demonstrates the power of small actions and individual choices even in the face of overwhelming odds.

In "The Star Thrower," a solitary man walks along a beach littered with stranded starfish that have washed ashore and are dying in the sand. The narrator encounters a second man, a stranger, who lifts a struggling starfish out of the sand and throws it carefully back out into the sea. The stranger invites the narrator to join him in saving the starfish. "Throw well. One can help them," he says. The narrator is skeptical. It seems to him this is a pointless task; there are too many dying starfish and one man cannot save them all. Later, however, the narrator realizes that the star thrower's efforts *do* matter. They matter to the individual starfish, to *each one* that is saved. He finds the star thrower again and joins him, saying, "Call me another thrower." The narrator concludes, "After us, there will be others….We had kept, some of us, the memory of the perfect circle of compassion from life to death and back to life again— the completion of the rainbow of existence."[41]

Beginning this practice is a little thing that matters. In taking this first step, you have become a "star thrower" yourself, one who remembers that "perfect circle of compassion." You have opened the channel for the very best of yourself to find expression, voice, and movement in this world. *Little things matter* and you are not a little thing. You are my dearest hope for this world; you are a friend I have not met yet; you are the creator of your own movement; and you are my neighbor in the Blue. Together, we can transform life on this planet, single action by single action. Let your spiral begin!

---

40 To read more about Loren Eiseley, see https://en.wikipedia.org/wiki/Loren_Eiseley.
41 Loren Eiseley, *The Unexpected Universe* (Orlando, FL: Hartcourt Brace & Company, 1969), 91.

Summary:
The Exercises and Movements

A Breath of Fresh Air

1. *Close your eyes and turn your attention to your breath. At first, simply notice your breath, allowing it to flow in and out of you naturally, at your own pace. Do this for a minute or so.*

2. *On your next inhalation, draw a long, steady breath deep into your lungs. Fill your lungs from the bottom upward, from deep in your belly to the top of your throat. At the top of the breath, hold the breath for a count of 1-2-3-4. Now, slowly release the breath from the top down, emptying your lungs slowly from throat to belly. Visually, it is helpful to picture in your mind's eye a tall glass being filled to the top with water, then the glass being tilted and slowly emptied. Any time you are having trouble keeping your focus on the breath, repeat this visualization of the glass being slowly filled with water and emptied.*

3. *Return to your own natural pace of breathing for a moment, gently noticing the natural rise and fall of your chest. As you do so, take a moment to express gratitude for the precious gift of your breath.*

Steps 2 and 3 may be repeated as many times as you wish. Be sure to end the exercise with a moment of gratitude for the wonderful, life-giving resource that is your own, unique breath.

Awareness of Big Mama Earth

1 **Notice and Tell**

One of the things my sister taught me is that you don't have to allow for a lot of free time in order to appreciate nature. It is something you can bring into each of your days, no matter how busy you are, and you don't have to go on a long nature hike to do it. My sister would use the time she spent driving into town to really notice (while driving safely, of course!) the beautiful Pennsylvania country scenery.

If you live in the city, notice a tree-lined street or rooftop garden. If you are doing some highway driving, take note of the landscape or perhaps a beautiful cloud formation in the sky. Or simply notice a flower box someone has planted—that is, after all, why he or she planted it!

2 Get Out Into It All
When you do have a little free time, why not spend it outside? Take a weekend hike or walk in the park. Don't have weekend time? Use a few minutes of your lunch break to stroll around the block or park or eat in an outdoor café. While you are out there in nature, use the time to really look around you and notice the beauty the world has to offer, then go tell someone!

3 Buy a Potted Plant or Flower or Look Out the Window
Even if you can't get outside, you can bring nature to you. Get a potted plant or flower, or have someone bring you one. Or simply look out of the window and take note. Even a rainy or snowy day has natural beauty. Spend a few conscious moments everyday observing some aspect of nature that is pleasant to your eyes and/or ears.

Don't forget to share what you see, hear and feel with someone else! If you make this a habit, you are going to get excited about all the restorative powers of nature and want to share.

A Visualization Exercise

In your mind's eye, see yourself reaching out and opening the door you use the most to enter your home. When you have a good and detailed picture of your hand on the doorknob of the door, imagine opening the door and walking to your refrigerator. Now picture yourself opening the refrigerator door and taking out an orange. Feel the texture of the orange and smell the sweet oil of the fruit's skin. See yourself picking up a knife and cutting the orange into smiles. Feel the knife cutting into the orange and the juice on your hands. Pick up an orange smile and put it into your mouth and bite it so that when you smile your teeth show the skin of the orange.

If you are not a fan of oranges, you can do the exercise with any food you happen to love in your refrigerator!

Right-Brain Relaxation

1. *Choose a comfortable position and close your eyes. Relax every muscle in your body beginning with your toes and moving upward one muscle at a time through your feet, legs, pelvis, stomach, chest, shoulders, arms, neck, jaw, eyes, head, and face. Continue to breathe deeply and regularly at a comfortable pace.*
2. *When you think you are relaxed, release another layer of tension all over your entire body.*
3. *Move your awareness over your body again from toe to head. Wherever you sense tension, allow yourself to release it.*
4. *Repeat the entire relaxation three times. Each time you begin to think, "I am as relaxed as I can get," let go of another layer of tension.*
5. *Now, feel where you are in the space—physically and mentally. Feel your connection with Mother Earth. Where does your body touch solidness and where does it come into contact with air?*
6. *In your mind's eye, visualize yourself expanding like a firework in all directions, deep into the Earth and out into space at the same time. Like a rubber band, snap yourself back into your body.*

Repeat the last step several times, becoming huge and encompassing everything, then snapping back into your own body. Coming back into your body gives you a point of reference where you can feel grounded if at any time you feel too spacey during the exercise.

Clear Heart Meditation

1. *Choose a comfortable place where you feel quite safe. If possible, play some relaxing instrumental music in the background while you do the meditation exercise. Make sure the music does not have lyrics that might distract you. Arrange yourself in a comfortable position, either*

seated or lying down, so that your whole body feels supported by the surface beneath you.

2. *Begin by relaxing your mind and body with some deep breathing. Inhale deeply and visualize your body being filled with a blue wave of fresh, clean air, all the way from the crown of your head down to your toes. As you slowly exhale, imagine that the blue wave is sweeping any stress or anxiety from your body so that you can release it. Breathe in this way for several moments, allowing your body to relax and feel supported by the surface beneath you. On each inhalation, you are allowing the wave to gather up any tension or discomfort or nagging thoughts. You then release them completely on the exhale, until you reach a place of mental and physical relaxation.*

3. *Once you feel comfortable and relaxed, allow your breath to return to an even, natural rhythm, breathing at whatever pace is comfortable for you. Now, turn your attention to the area of your heart, simply noticing how it feels. Your heart chakra may feel warm and soft and open, or it may feel tense or tight or restricted. However it feels, try to simply notice the feeling without judgment. If it is comforting to you, you may wish to place one or both of your hands over your heart. Just take a moment here to honor how this part of you is feeling, whatever that may be for you in this moment, knowing the feelings here change all the time. Remind yourself that your heart is your oldest friend, it has been with you through thick and thin, and it will always be there for you, no matter what.*

4. *Now, see if you can speak directly to your heart. Either aloud or in your mind, say the following words: "Thank you for being a steady and faithful companion. Thank you for carrying all that you have carried. Now, I am ready to release the things that no longer serve me. Thank you." Make sure you express each word slowly and deliberately. Afterward, simply continue to breathe gently—in and out—noticing whatever comes up without judgment. You may feel a sensation of release or a feeling of resistance, but whatever comes up, there is no need to force anything. Simply notice the feeling. You may repeat the*

message once or twice if it feels right to do so.

5. *When you are ready, express a thought of gratitude to your heart, knowing it will always be with you and it can grow and change with you as well. Next, inhale deeply to bring yourself out of the clear heart meditation. At your own pace, emerge from your state of relaxation by wiggling your fingers and toes and stretching your muscles. Now, open your eyes. Finally, bring your hands together in a prayer position over your heart. Bowing your head over your hands, express a final "thank you," to your heart, to yourself, to Mother Earth, and to the Divine Universe for being your generous and loving resources.*

Illuminate Also My Heart

Every individual experiences Love, Service, and Gratitude differently, and the ways in which your connection to these true states plays out in your own life are totally unique. Writing this book and sharing the Spiral Blueprint Meditation is one of the ways Love, Service, and Gratitude have manifested in my life, but you will undoubtedly find you are inspired in other ways.

New creative projects might occur to you, or you may find more healing and forgiveness opening up in your personal relationships. Maybe you will have new ideas about the work you do, or maybe you will discover new business opportunities or financial resources. As you reconnect with the unbreakable loop of Love, Service, and Gratitude, your vibration is raised in such a way that you can attract and draw new possibilities for good things into your life. You begin acting from your truest, deepest self, so that your efforts and actions will emerge naturally from this place.

The prayer, "You who are the source of all power, whose rays illuminate the whole world, illuminate also my heart so that it too can do your Work" is associated with Sowelu, the ancient rune representing the creative, life-giving properties of the sun.[42] In his book *The Rune Cards: Ancient Wisdom for the New Millennium*, Ralph Blum includes a visualization with this prayer that I also suggest as a supplemental exercise. Prayer and mantra are powerful aids to help us focus our minds as we visualize healing and connection. From the place of healing and

42 Blum, The Rune Cards, 154.

connection, we then bravely begin to manifest our own best, authentic selves. This supplementary visualization and prayer is a good way to welcome healing and creativity into your heart, and also invite the brilliant manifestations that are sure to come once you have done so!

Prayer to the Sun Rune Exercise

> *1. Recite the words of the prayer, either out loud or in your mind:*
> - *You who are the source of all power*
> - *Whose rays illuminate the whole world,*
> - *Illuminate also my heart*
> - *So that it too can do your Work.*
> *2. As you do so, visualize the light of the sun pouring into your heart, flowing through your body and into the Earth beneath you, then traveling back out and into the world around you. Repeat the prayer three times if you wish.*[43]

From here, Love, Service, and Gratitude emerge naturally. As you begin to act from this place of wholeness and connection, you will naturally be operating at your highest level. Your authentic self can take over, radiating Gratitude and Service from within and rippling out into the world around you in your actions. Love, Service and Gratitude provide a meaningful path, but the meaning of this will be different to each of you.

Releasing Fear Meditation

One of the most common negative feelings we tend to hold is the emotion of fear. We fear the future, we fear our failures, and we fear death. Releasing fear is an important part of keeping your personal torus clear. The following meditation exercise is from Brad Austen, an intuitive meditation teacher trained in Psychic Development and Mediumship, and can be found on YouTube.[44]

This exercise is simple and can be practiced virtually anytime, anywhere. Use it as a

43 Ibid., 155.
44 Brad Austen, "Releasing Fear Meditation (Guided Meditation)," March 28, 2015, https://www.youtube.com/watch?v=HdFGGjxzyOo.

supplementary meditation exercise to help you practice releasing the primary negative emotion of fear.

1. *Begin by calling on the light, Archangel Michael, God or whatever you perceive it to be. Take a deep breath in and exhale gently.*
2. *Become aware of the speed of your breathing. By breathing deeply and slowly, your body and mind gradually relax.*
3. *Take another deep breath in and exhale gently.*

Visualize a violet transmuting laser of light coming down into your crown at the top of your head. See this laser zapping away any negativity, any fear-based energies. This violet laser of light is transmuting any fear-based energy that may be affecting you now.

4. *Keep calling on the light to transmute your fears now, whatever they may be.*

Fear can manifest in different ways: phobias, fears or repetitive habits. See this violet light transmuting your fears and returning them to neutral energy.

Within a few minutes, your fear or anxiety will reduce and become more manageable.

5. *Ask the light to seal your aura and visualize your aura becoming clear and strong.*
6. *If you are still feeling some fear at this point, visualize the fear-based energies bouncing off your aura. This energy can no longer penetrate your aura and body.*
7. *Ask the light to take away any energy or entities not for your highest good.*
8. *Ask the light to remove these energies from you on a full and permanent basis now.*
9. *Finally, visualize the violet light sealing your aura with light and protection, so that only love-based energies may enter your field.*
10. *If you can, try to hold a happy or joy-filled emotion in your heart.*
11. *Allow this feeling to expand out from your heart and expand throughout your entire body and aura.*

12. Thank the light for helping you during your time of need.
13. Remember that we have free will. Spirit respects our free will, and so we need to ask for assistance when required.

Whenever you feel anxious or fearful, remember to practice this meditation exercise. Over time, your fears will lessen and become more manageable, but it does require effort and practice.

Connecting With Your Power

9. To begin, find a comfortable position, either seated or standing, where you can feel your feet in contact with the ground. It is important to feel grounded for this meditation exercise, so if possible, avoid a reclined or cross-legged position. Consciously bring your awareness to your feet or to your lower body, taking a moment to be aware of your solid connection to the Earth.

10. Now, practice a simple cleansing breath cycle: inhale deeply as you count to four; hold the in-breath for the counts of five and six; then exhale completely and hold the breath out for counts seven and eight. Repeat this cycle several times for two minutes or so, focusing on the breath and allowing your body to relax and your mind to become clear of other concerns.

11. Allow your breath to return to a natural, comfortable rhythm. Bring your awareness to your third chakra. Take a moment to simply notice, without judgment, how this area feels right now. A color may appear to you as well. Simply take note of the color, without judgment. Accept whatever comes up. If it feels right to do so, you may place one or both of your hands over the power chakra.

12. Now, see if you can visualize your power chakra becoming a warm shade of orange, deep yellow or orange-red. Think of the warmth of the sun on a clear summer day. Visualize the color of such a sun and see if you can bring that warmth into your power chakra.

13. Either aloud or in your mind, repeat the following mantra: "This

is mine. This is my power. I am in my power, and I am grateful."

14.   *Now imagine a radiant light, red or orange or deep yellow, streaming forward from this place and suffusing your entire body.*

15.   *Visualize the streaming rays of light coming gradually back down into your third chakra, until they are contained once more as a gently glowing orb of light.*

16.   *Breathe in deeply once more and gradually exhale. Slowly open your eyes and bring your awareness back into the world around you.*

Throughout your day, you can periodically bring your awareness back to that glowing orb of light at your third chakra and see if you can imagine yourself acting from this place. Whenever you do this, also take a moment to feel your feet on the ground or to feel the connection between your lower body (below the power chakra) and the Earth.

Compassion Visualization
(an extension of the Clear Heart Meditation)

1. *Begin by finding a comfortable position. You can practice this seated, standing, or lying down, whatever feels most comfortable to you.*

2. *Take a moment to attune to your breath, breathing in deeply and evenly, and exhaling slowly and evenly. As you inhale, gather up any tension in your body, and release it on the exhale. After a few cycles, allow your breath to return to a natural, even rhythm.*

3. *Next, turn your attention to your heart chakra. First, simply notice if there are any particular feelings or even colors that come to you as you do so. Honor whatever you notice, without judgment, while continuing to breathe easily and naturally.*

4. *Now, visualize a warm, golden light filling your heart chakra. Imagine the light is literally compassion itself. Allow the light to flow outward from your heart, radiating like the rays of the sun. Allow this radiance to flow throughout your entire body, to the top of your head, and to the tips of your fingers and toes.*

5. *Imagine the golden rays streaming outward from your body, all*

around you and out into the Universe. Visualize the light flowing further and further out, up, and down into the Earth beneath you, connecting everything in an endless, shimmering web of compassion.

6. *Finally, place your hands in prayer position over the center of your chest and bow your head slightly. Either aloud or in your mind, repeat the following mantra: "Compassion, always and everywhere, for myself, and all that is."*

7. *When you are ready, slowly open your eyes and ease your awareness back into the world around you.*

The Complete Spiral Blueprint Meditation

To begin with, I ask that you create an intention. This might be something as simple as "I am loved" or "The change is within me." Feel free to use one of these or come up with your own simple intention. Just go with whatever is in your heart.

Take a moment to focus on your intention. As you do so, imagine that you are connecting your energy with the energy of the universe and grounding your energy in the Earth. Remember, you are creating the foundation for many other intentions in this Meditation.

Now, perform the following nine motions of the Spiral Blueprint Meditation in continuous movement:

*(**Note**: As in Tai Chi, fluidity of movement is more important than exact steps. Be mindful of your movements, but do not worry about doing them perfectly.)*

1. *Stand with your feet shoulder-width apart, knees slightly bent, back straight, and arms at your side. If needed, you may sit in a chair with your back straight and arms resting at your sides or on your lap. Even if you are completely immobile, you can imagine the steps in your mind's eye. The effects will be the same. Your intention is to be in the present moment, in mind and body. Relaxing your mind and body, become aware of how you feel and of your surroundings. Become aware of your breathing in...and out.*

2. Relax by taking three deep breaths, inhaling deeply and exhaling slowly. With each exhale, relax your body from head to toe. If necessary, keep taking slow deep breaths a little longer than three times. Just breathe in and out until you are fully relaxed, jaw and shoulders soft, and all tension is released throughout your entire body. As you breathe, slowly become aware of the sounds around you. Notice the smells. Become mindful of how you physically feel: peaceful and energized or in pain and tired. Simply become aware—without judgment—of the environment and how your body feels in this moment, but don't think about the connections you have to these things. Relax and allow yourself to simply be aware. If you feel yourself starting to think, judge or worry, return your attention to your breathing. Focusing on even one breath can help you to become mindful again.

3. Bring your hands up slowly from the sides of your body, cupping your palms up in front of you, with elbows slightly bent. Visualize pulling up two handfuls of the energy of Mother Earth, the way you would scoop up a draught of water in your cupped palms. Hold the energy out and up slightly as an offering. As you make this gesture, imagine you are pulling from deep within Mother Earth all her strength, calmness and restorative energy. Give thanks for her gifts.

4. While you are holding your cupped hands up, offer the gifts of Mother Earth and your gratitude to the Universe. Visualize brilliant colors—red, orange, yellow, green, blue, and purple flowing into your cupped hands from the creative center of the galaxy. Once your cupped hands are filled to overflowing, the intense colors transform into a luminous white light that overflows, like a waterfall from your hands. Both the energies—the energy from Mother Earth and the brilliant creative energy of the Divine Universe—mix and fall back to Mother Earth through their most powerful conductor: you. Give thanks to the Universe for this energy.

5. Bring your hands to your heart—right hand on your heart first and then left hand over your right hand. You are preparing to absorb both

energies of Mother Earth and the Divine Universe into your heart, but first you must recognize and draw out all negativity. Visualize taking all the negative energy, thoughts, and feelings in both your conscious and subconscious mind into your left hand. This creates a path for all negativity to flow out of your body so that a new pathway to your heart can open.

6. *Speak the mantra, "Unconditional Universal Love, Unconditional Universal Service, Unconditional Universal Gratitude." As you say these words, keep your hands on your heart and visualize the brilliant white creative light of the Divine Universe and the dense, protective energy of Mother Earth flowing into your heart through your right hand. Concentrate on allowing these energies to fill every cell in your body clearing a path to Unconditional Love, Service, and Gratitude.*

7. *Keep your feet in place, and turn to the left as far as is comfortable. As you turn, drop your left hand toward the ground—palm down—and release all known and unknown negativity into Mother Earth where it can be received and cleansed. The action will look and feel like you are slowly throwing what isn't needed anymore out onto the ground behind you. As you prepare to perform the next motion, keep your left palm open and positioned behind you.*

8. *While your left hand stays open behind you, gently readjust your left hand, but keep it open and slowly turn your upper body to the right as far as is comfortable for you. Think of it as a flowing Tai Chi movement. As you turn to the right, reach your right hand up toward the sky like you are picking an apple off a tree from a ladder and the apple is behind you. Your right hand is now cupped, palm up, and ready to accept all the positive healing energy of the Universe.*

9. *Visualize pure white light falling like a warm, wonderful shower, as you soak pure love and healing energy deep into every cell in your body. Imagine a warm blanket of protection coming up from the Earth and completely surrounding you with refreshing, beautiful and creative energy. Let that energy flow into your right hand, through your body, and then down toward Mother Earth through your left*

hand. *Repeat the same meditative motions using your opposite side.*

10. *At the end of each repetition, visualize an explosion of pure white, loving light bursting forth from you in all directions, out into the Universe, surrounding and covering the Earth. Like the twist in your DNA and the loop of your personal torus, you have created and aligned yourself with the pure energy of Unconditional Universal Love, Unconditional Universal Service, and Unconditional Universal Gratitude.*

11. *Slowly turn and face forward. All in one movement, bring your right hand to your heart. Bring your left hand up to cover your right hand. Tap your heart three times. Repeat on the opposite side.*

About the Author

L. Bogedin grew up in and still lives tucked into the quiet scenic bend of the Susquehanna River in rural Northeastern Pennsylvania. Lori does most of her writing at home with her husband, three dogs and their crazy cat. She submitted a story chosen for Brian Weiss's 2012 book "Miracles Happen" and also wrote a short story about her three adopted girls for a book due out in early 2016. Lori wrote and self-published a children's book called, "Warm Fuzzies". A heartfelt book inspired by the love for her grandson that threaten to overwhelm her empty heart. Her next project is a children's series called, "The Adventures of Terrance A. Dragon".

Bibliography

1 "Quoteworthy Science," APS News, http://www.aps.org/publications/apsnews/199904/quoteworthy.cfm.

1 Gregg Braden, *The Spontaneous Healing of Belief: Shattering the Paradigm of False Limits* (Carlsbad, CA: Hay House, 2008), iii.

3 Ibid.

1 To read Lorenz's paper in its entirety, see http://eaps4.mit.edu/research/Lorenz/Butterfly_1972.pdf.

1 John Wesley, "The Character of a Methodist," *The Works of John Wesley* (Thomas Jackson edition, 1872), http://www.umcmission.org/Find-Resources/John-Wesley-Sermons/The-Wesleys-and-Their-Times/The-Character-of-a-Methodist.

1 Leonard Cohen "Anthem," http://genius.com/2001798/Leonard-cohen-anthem/There-is-a-crack-a-crack-in-everything-thats-how-the-light-gets-in.

1 Matthew 7:7.

1 Eckhart Tolle, *The Power of Now: A Guide to Spiritual Enlightenment* (Novato, CA: New World Library, 1999), 58.

1 Jill Bolte Taylor, "My Stroke of Insight," Ted2008, http://www.ted.com/talks/jill_bolte_taylor_s_powerful_stroke_of_insight?language=en.

1 To view Dr. Emoto's documentary, see http://www.cultureunplugged.com/play/8141/Messages-from-Water.

1 Tolle, *The Power of Now*.

1 Deepak Chopra, *The Path to Love: Spiritual Strategies for Healing* (New York, NY: Three Rivers Press, 1997), 71.

1 Adapted from http://ancientearthwarriors.com/tag/sioux-legend/.

1 Adapted from https://yourdailyprayer.wordpress.com/tag/lakota/.

1 For more quotes from Ralph Waldo Emerson, see http://www.goodreads.com/quotes/14250-to-a-dull-mind-all-of-nature-is-leaden-to.

1 Marco Bischof, *Biophotons—The Light in Our Cells* (Frankfurt, Germany: Zweitausendeins, 1995).

www.ingramcontent.com/pod-product-compliance
Lightning Source LLC
Chambersburg PA
CBHW080523030426
42337CB00023B/4614